THE CALL
FOR CHARACTER

RETURNING to the TRUE NATURE of PROPHETIC MINISTRY

TROY KROMBHOLZ

THE CALL For CHARACTER
Returning to the True Nature of Prophetic Ministry

A Master Press Cover Design

THE CALL For CHARACTER
Returning to the True Nature of Prophetic Ministry

ISBN 978-0-9646543-6-5
For information:

MASTER PRESS
3405 ISLAND BAY WAY, KNOXVILLE, TN 37931
Mail to: publishing@ masterpressbooks.com

Acknowledgments

Thank you Jesus first and foremost for giving me the privilege

to carry the burden of this message to others!

Your steadfast love and long-suffering with this weak vessel is

one of the greatest joys a man can know.

Jesus, may your name be glorified in all the earth! Amen

Secondly to my wife Susan,

who has lovingly and with great sacrifice tithed her husband

for the completion of this project.

You are a jewel among many women and

an example to me by your sacrifice!

Thirdly to Ray & Catherine, Wilbur & Jan, and Erick

your support has caused this work to go forward

to minister to the Kingdom of God.

May the fruit of your hands

bless you over and over all the years of your life!

BOOK REVIEWS

We are living in a time where the church's ministry is being used for just about every other reason except for what it was meant to do...to build and establish the body of Christ on earth. Because of this, much of the church has become weak, blind, and prone to disease. The desperate need of the hour is for us to turn back to our Biblical blueprint, and with humility, honesty, and faith in the wisdom of God, allow Him to correct us. What God will produce won't be glamorous or attractive by this world's standards but it will be genuine and the gates of hell will not prevail against it. A clarion call for purity and holiness in ministry, I believe (this book) can be beneficial for any church ministry. Written with clarity and filled with redemptive love, may it be another tool used by God to prepare Himself a Bride without spot or wrinkle.

Dale Schmucker Lead Singer
Hopesong Music Group

This is a great book for any Christian that desires to be sharpened by God's Word, including those who serve in Prophetic Ministry. In our present deteriorating culture we must hold onto the truth in God's word. This book lets scripture speak for itself. It is a refreshing and gentle call back to purity and holiness that the Church desperately needs.

Tim Taylor
Worship Team Musician
Richland Creek Community Church
Wake Forest, North Carolina

This is a very timely message for the church as Troy Krombholz takes us through a very neglected function of the church; true Spirit led prophecy. I find "The Call for Character" very easy to read and yet very meaty and challenging. Troy uses a lot of Scripture throughout the book with real true life stories woven in, to give meaning and application. It was a real blessing for me to read and I will say, find some answers to some of my own searching. Although Troy's heart here is mainly on prophecy, he paints a very biblical and down to earth picture of living and walking a Spirit led life, not only in the function of the local church, but also in our daily walk as Christians. I encourage all Christians to read "The Call for Character", and believe this could be a key to revival in the church.

Nathan Nissley, pastor

El Dorado Springs, MO

Introduction

One of the original teachers of Martin Luther said the following, "We preach what we need (to) learn most!" That in many ways serves as the inspiration of this book. Several years ago I felt a calling on my life towards full time ministry. Yet, I had no clue how to get there with what I knew at that time. There were so many aspects of spiritual gifts and "The Five Fold Ministry" I did not feel educated about. When I say "The Five Fold Ministry" I am referring to Ephesians 4 that reveals the 5 main arms of church ministry: apostles, prophets, evangelists, pastors and teachers. So over many years I pursued discipleship with different churches, ministries, and Bible schools, seemingly to no avail.

For me I felt a calling early on specifically towards prophetic ministry, though I struggled to find answers to my own questions. However there were not many including my own mentors, who were genuinely teaching on this type of ministry from a true Biblical perspective. Many of my lessons were learned through trial and error. The problem is that there is quite the lack of good education on this topic. God in his mercy continued to keep His hand on me, to teach and to guide me. The question I kept on asking over and over again was this, "How does prophetic ministry truly function within the New Covenant community?"

This is a very hard topic to understand because of our current problems in the church body. There are many abuses of prophetic ministry in the Liberal side of Christianity, and a horrible negligent use of prophetic ministry in the Reformed side of Christianity. So after much dismay in many different seasons, I began to ask God what His word says about prophetic ministry. This is where my journey began to write this book on prophetic ministry.

When the church body doesn't provide the answers you seek, it causes you to return to the source for the answers, The Word of God. So I began to ask God the questions I needed answers for, and this is where true life began to flow. Not long after I started this project, the answers and information flooded my way at lightning speed. Over the course of writing this book, I experienced mighty confirmations from numerous different preachers, sermons, and classes. I knew without a doubt, this topic needed to go forth to encourage others called to this ministry.

This book's intention is to educate, inform, and encourage those who feel they have a prophetic calling in their life. No matter whether you are young or old, male or female, God has prophetic ministers intended to be used in the body of Christ for its edification! The goal of this book is to help temper and train us, so that we all function correctly in the body of Christ. Prophetic ministry though often misunderstood, is still active today! Although I feel the urgency to write this book to people who are called to prophetic ministry, many of these chapters are fully applicable to all ministers and followers of Jesus Christ. We all can learn from it, and my prayer is that you will have ears to hear the message.

As the author of this book I wish to make it clear to you what this book is, and what this book is not. This book is not a bitter, backbiting, stab at the body of Christ first and foremost. Nor does the book intend to slander any particular denomination(s), schools, or any para-church ministry. I am just trying to encourage you how to do prophetic ministry right, not spend an entire book bashing those who are doing it wrong! The intention of this book is to teach and show you how to use prophetic ministry correctly in the body of Christ. Furthermore this book is not as much about the manifestations of New Covenant prophecy, as much as it is about the heart, tone, and outcome of prophecy! To accomplish this I had to submerge myself in the Word of God to get the real answers.

That being said, it is my intention to speak truthfully when issues or matters come up in this book that expose a failure in the body. It is my intention to speak truthfully and tenderly with all the information that I provide in this book. A well known preacher operating in the body of Christ, said the following, "Don't curse the darkness, instead light a candle!" It is my intention to light a candle with this book, and not to curse the darkness at work.

This book is a passionate study for me as a writer, and much of the information researched comes from my personal classroom with the Lord. I cannot say that all of my questions are answered, nor can I say that I will answer all of yours. However in writing this book I can at least open the topic of true prophetic ministry in the New Covenant, and by doing so shine a light on the Narrow Path that this ministry walks on. It is my hope to paint a large canvas to reveal the heart and tone of a prophetic individual clearly.

This book will address also, some dangers that prophetic ministry experiences against it, and how to respond when those attacks come at you. This book serves as a checklist for your own personal journey in learning. As a check list it will show you what things need to be in place if you are going to follow the Lord's call on your life in this manner. It is my earnest hope and intention with this book to provide you with encouragement, and good seeds from the Lord how to walk in your calling!

Through the agony of much pain, and in many trials; some of which have a mighty victory, and some of which have utter defeat, this work, has endured the excruciating pains of labor, and by the grace of God will be used to plant many seeds of life, for the Glory of Jesus Christ, my forerunner in the agony of pain, and ultimately in the end... His TRIUMPH! Blessings to you in the name of Jesus Christ, and be encouraged with this book!

—Troy Krombholz

TABLE OF CONTENTS

SECTION ONE

Laying the Foundation of Prophecy

SECTION TWO

Victory in the Anointed Tongue

TABLE OF CONTENTS

SECTION THREE

Dangers to the Prophetic Calling

SECTION FOUR

Anointed Eyes–Seeing the Big Picture

Section 1

Laying the Foundation of Prophecy

Discovering the Fervent Unction
That God Will Give You

The purpose of section one which includes the first five chapters is to reveal the foundations and heart of true prophetic ministry. Each of these chapters intertwines and reveals the heart of God. When you are open to the heart of God, he will lay the groundwork for these truths in your life. Though not in sequential order, these chapters are essential, so that we will function correctly as prophetic ministers in the body of Christ. These are the foundations of prophecy!

1. The Father Burns for Righteousness in the Temple

2. The Fear of the Lord

3. The Zeal of the Lord

4. The Prophetic Sigh

5. God's Authority and Order

CHAPTER ONE

The Father Burns for Righteousness in the Temple

In the beginning it was GOOD! This included the relationship that God had with his children Adam and Eve. He waited on them every day for their walks in the garden. He walked and talked with them in such a dear and awesome way. He delighted in them and their quality fellowship. They were intimate with the Lord, and he had unhindered relationship with them. But the devil despised this relationship, and came on a mission to destroy it. Adam and Eve then sinned which broke that sweet fellowship with God, and they were no longer righteous.

The need for prophetic ministry started when Adam and Eve ate the forbidden fruit, and sold themselves as slaves to the dominion of the devil and his kingdom of rebellion. No longer could God stand holding the hands of man as he once did. He now had to separate himself from their un-holiness. The heart of prophetic ministry started before the foundations of the earth. God needed a way to relate once again with his sheep, so the Word of God, Jesus Himself started the prophetic ministry, and knew ahead of time what he would say and do to redeem a fallen people. The voice of the Prophetic Ministry started with a theological term called, "Protoevangelium". Protoevangelium simply means, "The First Gospel". This Gospel is found in the following passage:

"...I will put enmity between you and the woman, and between your offspring and her offspring; he shall bruise your head, and you shall bruise his heel."

Genesis 3:15

Clearly this statement of prophecy is one of the first, if not the very first places in the Bible where God prophesied the redemption and restoration of a fallen people. The Father's heart burned for righteousness to be restored to his lost sheep. God is an absolutely HOLY God, there is no darkness found in him, nor any sin, weakness or failure. When mankind sinned and ate the fruit, they no longer had pure, clear fellowship with God. From that point forward God's plan of redemption started to manifest itself. In essence, God in heaven said to the son Jesus, Son, Go and get my people back from the devil! Hallelujah! Even in the passage in Genesis as listed above, God was already showing his intentions through the means of the cross. So in the Old Covenant the work began to draw the hearts of his lost children back to him. Who are his lost children? We are all, and were.

For although they knew God, they did not honor him as God or give thanks to him, but they became futile in their thinking, and their foolish hearts were darkened. Claiming to be wise, they became fools, and exchanged the glory of the immortal God for images resembling mortal man and birds and animals and reptiles.

Therefore God gave them up in the lusts of their hearts to impurity, to the dishonoring of their bodies among themselves, because they exchanged the truth about God for a lie and worshiped and served the creature rather than the Creator, who is blessed forever! Amen.

For this reason God gave them up to dishonorable passions. For their women exchanged natural relations for those that are contrary to nature;

Romans 1:21-26

The Old Covenant in the fewest of words bears the heart of the Father pointing to Jesus. Clearly in the Old Covenant the blood of bulls and goats could never take away the sin nature; it served only as a type and a covering for sin. Yet there are many people who may ask, "Why was Jesus not sent sooner?" For me personally, as I have pondered this, it seems both logical and heartfelt that man would be given a chance to see their need of a pure Savior. Man likes to fix his own problems and God in his long-suffering gave man time to prove his inability to take away sins by themselves. So in a sense, God let man come to his end of futile striving and workings to nothingness. Yet all the while God desired righteousness, even though he only received it through the veil. So many times we think how they had to look at God through a veil, and the relationship was hindered. But, it is very interesting to look at it from God's point of view staring at us through that veil, wanting to have genuine fellowship with us again, walking in the garden together. God from the beginning wanted a restored relationship, and sin hindered it.

So how does God, who loves his lost sheep reach them? He sends anointed ministers including prophets to speak forth his words. The entire Old Covenant is full of these anointed prophets responsible for carrying the word of the Lord to lost sheep. Throughout the Old Testament there are many occasions that prophets seem violent or vicious against sinners, and lawless people. But as reminder to all who read this, it was God who set the standard of the law for the people to follow. Granted there were additional traditions and ordinances placed by Moses, and the leaders that followed, that became extra burdens on the people. God wanted a Holy People at his criteria, but man wanted to be holy by his own criteria. So some may say, "God was such an angry God in the Old Testament, and slaughtered everyone without cause."

To that I say emphatically consider the following verses:

> *The soul who sins shall die. The son shall not suffer for the iniquity of the father, nor the father suffer for the iniquity of the son. The righteousness of the righteous shall be upon himself, and the wickedness of the wicked shall be upon himself.*

> *But if a wicked person turns away from all his sins that he has committed and keeps all my statutes and does what is just and right, he shall surely live; he shall not die. None of the transgressions that he has committed shall be remembered against him; for the righteousness that he has done he shall live. Have I any pleasure in the death of the wicked, declares the Lord God, and not rather that he should turn from his way and live?*
>
> *Ezekiel 18:20-23*

And again we see him repeat himself in the following verses:

> *"Therefore I will judge you, O house of Israel, every one according to his ways, declares the Lord God. Repent and turn from all your transgressions, lest iniquity be your ruin. Cast away from you all the transgressions that you have committed, and make yourselves a new heart and a new spirit! Why will you die, O house of Israel? For I have no pleasure in*

the death of anyone, declares the Lord God; so turn, and live."

Ezekiel 18:30-32

So at this point if you are asking if God is an unkind God, or an unloving God, you will see by his very own words that he does not like it at all when anyone unrighteous dies. Furthermore these following verses confirm it through his son Jesus, when he was obedient to the Father to come and rescue the lost sheep.

For God so loved the world, that he gave his only Son, that whoever believes in him should not perish but have eternal life. For God did not send his Son into the world to condemn the world, but in order that the world might be saved through him. Whoever believes in him is not condemned, but whoever does not believe is condemned already, because he has not believed in the name of the only Son of God.

John 3:16-18

Therefore the Old Covenant was used to set the stage as a preparation for the New Covenant and Saving Power of Jesus Christ. Because, as the following verses say; we all need to hear the preacher.

For "everyone who calls on the name of the Lord will be saved."

But how are they to call on him in whom they have not believed? And how are they to believe in him of whom they have never heard? And how are they to hear without someone preaching? And how are they to preach unless they are sent? As it is written, "How beautiful are the feet of those who preach the good news!"

Rom 10:13-15

So even though prophetic ministry was the base and common practice in the Old Covenant for the people, prophetic individuals could never serve as their Savior... though in the process they were still pointing to the Savior and the relationship of the Father, by the power of the Holy Spirit. The heart and origins of prophetic ministry started in the father's longing for a restored righteous family! In all cases in the Old Covenant when prophetic men, and or anointed individuals saw an angel of the Lord, the angels informed them not to bow down to them, because they were not Jesus. Even the angels know not to receive praise from men, only the Lord was to receive praise from men. All forms of Old and New Covenant life points to Jesus as the scriptures says:

> Then I fell down at his feet to worship him, but he said
> to me, "You must not do that! I am a fellow servant with you
> and your brothers who hold to the testimony of Jesus. Worship
> God." For the testimony of Jesus is the spirit of prophecy.
>
> Revelation 19:10

The Old Covenant is filled with the communion and worship of God in a tabernacle and in a temple, because the tabernacle and temple were the only real places of fellowship between the Father and his children. Because of this limited space to relate with his children don't you think he is going to burn for its righteousness and cleanliness? So here enters Jesus! Jesus comes on the scene to fulfill the restoration of the lost sheep, yet he had to confront the problems that were present in the temple. This is where we see a really good glimpse of the Father's heart burning for righteousness, as seen in the New Covenant, through Jesus.

> The Passover of the Jews was at hand, and Jesus
> went up to Jerusalem. In the temple he found those who
> were selling oxen and sheep and pigeons, and the money-
> changers sitting there. And making a whip of cords, he
> drove them all out of the temple, with the sheep and oxen.

And he poured out the coins of the money-changers and overturned their tables. And he told those who sold the pigeons, "Take these things away; do not make my Father's house a house of trade." His disciples remembered that it was written, "Zeal for your house will consume me.

John 2:13-17

In each of the Gospels we see the harmony with this encounter of Jesus in the Temple. Each of them references these (3) following verses:

"... These I will bring to my holy mountain, and make them joyful in my house of prayer; their burnt offerings and their sacrifices will be accepted on my altar; for my house shall be called a house of prayer for all peoples."

Isaiah 56:7

Has this house, which is called by my name, become a den of robbers in your eyes? Behold, I myself have seen it, declares the LORD.

Jeremiah 7:11

For zeal for your house has consumed me, and the reproaches of those who reproach you have fallen on me.

Psalms 69:9

By looking at the preceding verses, and what Jesus did in the temple, one can easily conclude that the temple was a mess and without cleanliness. If we were standing on the corner of the temple garden and a man, (known as a prophet) came in and turned over all the tables, what would we think when we saw such a shocking act? Yet, Jesus was God himself, and also revealed the Father's heart here on earth. Jesus was the manifestation of the invisible Father God. Therefore the son desired for the Father to be respected in the way he deserved. Furthermore the son desired the Father's house to be treated in the way it should be treated. The focal point was the Physical Temple, and the conclusion at hand of the Old Covenant.

That being said, if Jesus burned in his heart for the cleanliness of the Physical Temple, so we as Prophetic Watchmen of the New Covenant should burn for the cleanliness of the Spiritual Temple. Now that Jesus died and granted us access to the Father in a restored relationship, we are the new temple.

What agreement has the temple of God with idols? For we are the temple of the living God; as God said,

> "I will make my dwelling among them and walk among
> them, and I will be their God, and they shall be my people..."
>
> 2 Corinthians 6:16

This is where the heart of New Covenant prophetic ministry starts its portion of the race. God the Father started it from the beginning, followed by the prophets portraying God's heart, followed by Jesus fulfilling the Father's heart, finalized by the prophetic ministry in the End Times, to complete the circle of pointing to Jesus.

Some say, "Well, prophetic ministry is not the same in the New Covenant." They say, "The office of prophet, or the works of prophets are not fulfilled in the same manner. We are under a New Covenant of Grace. Love people at all times, don't say such sharp words." We have all heard those statements and have chewed on them, but they are not the full picture. Knowing the full council of God means that he burns even today just as much as he did then, for the righteousness in His Temple. God does not change, and we are his temple. Therefore he will use prophets even still today, to speak to matters of unrighteousness.

Jesus is our righteousness and this is where our faith begins. We must burn to see people behold the lamb of God. This lamb is the one who takes away our sin, and gives us his righteousness. And all righteousness comes from the Father. God the father burns for people to walk in the righteousness of the Son, because his son was the only sacrifice that could be accepted for man's sin. The father's heart is all about Jesus. Therefore, prophetic ministry starts with Jesus and ends with Jesus, because the Testimony of Jesus IS the Spirit of Prophecy. Therefore as a caution to us all walking in this ministry, we need to remind ourselves of the following verses:

(Jesus Speaking....)"When the Spirit of truth comes, he will guide you into all the truth, for he will not speak on his own authority, but whatever he hears he will speak, and he will declare to you the things that are to come. He will glorify me, for he will take what is mine and declare it to you. All that the Father has is mine; therefore I said that he will take what is mine and declare it to you."

John 16:13-14

The above being said, take caution to anyone who claims to be walking by the Spirit in so called "Prophetic Ministry" if they do not glorify, reveal, or encourage you to be like Jesus, they may not be true prophets. So all prophecy, and prophetic utterance must point to Jesus and His testimony. The Testimony of Jesus is the Spirit of Prophecy.

We cannot walk in the prophetic calling except by the Spirit of God. Since therefore the Spirit of prophecy IS the testimony of Jesus, we therefore must know that testimony and let it embrace us well. We must have our own personal witness of the power of Jesus and his sacrifice if we are to walk in true prophecy. This true testimony of Jesus can only come when the Temple in each of us is continually being cleansed from all unrighteousness.

And he entered the temple and began to drive out those who sold, saying to them, "It is written, 'My house shall be a house of prayer,' but you have made it a den of robbers."

Luke 19:45-46

Jesus had to cleanse the physical temple because unrighteousness remained. He was ultimately pointing to the Spiritual Temple, in that "we" his temple must be walking by the Spirit free from unrighteousness. Anything of the flesh must be overthrown, because it hinders the work of God.

Prophetic ministry is all about Jesus receiving the reward of his suffering on the cross. His reward is having a bride, who walks in righteousness. Righteousness is consistent with God's nature. He desires everyone's life to be consistent with his nature, and true prophecy will always be consistent with God's nature. His nature is that of true righteousness, obtained by the blood of Jesus, and empowered by the Spirit. Jesus is the Alpha and Omega of Prophecy, because prophecy begins and ends with the testimony of Jesus! Therefore the Heart of the Father by using prophecy is pinpointed towards Jesus, the one he sent to redeem us from the dominion of sin and the devil. The Father has spoken through prophetic utterances since the beginning of time. Perhaps the question to ask is:, "Are we Listening?"

> *Then I fell down at his feet to worship him, but he said to me, "You must not do that! I am a fellow servant with you and your brothers who hold to the testimony of Jesus. Worship God." For the testimony of Jesus is the spirit of prophecy.*
> *Revelation 19:10*

Hallelujah!

CHAPTER TWO

The Fear of the Lord

The prophet's journey begins with the fear of the Lord... a true, holy, righteous fear of God. Now there are many people who do not understand what true fear of the Lord is, and in this chapter I would like to explain it clearly by scripture. Sadly, there are many who wrongly quote the following verse in regards to the Fear of the Lord, "Perfect love casts out all fear" (1 John 4:18). However, I wish to quickly let you know that verse is in the context of judgment for our works. This is where our works will be tested, and we should not fear that day. It is a very commonly used and misunderstood verse. However for the Christian and the prophet he will retain true Fear of The Lord! That is the purpose of this chapter.

First of all let's define the word fear by modern dictionaries, and other sources.

From Webster's 1828 Dictionary we read about fear:

"In scripture, fear is used to express a filial or a slavish passion. In good men, the fear of God is a holy awe or reverence of God and his laws, which springs from a just view and real love of the divine character, leading the subjects of it to hate and shun every thing that can offend such a holy being, and inclining them to aim at perfect obedience. This is filial fear."

"To feel a painful apprehension of some impending evil; to be afraid of; to consider or expect with emotions of alarm or solicitude. We fear the approach of an enemy or of a storm. We have reason to fear the punishment of our sins."

"Reverence; respect; due regard, to reverence; to have a reverential awe; to venerate."

"A painful emotion or passion excited by an expectation of evil, or the apprehension of impending danger. Fear expresses less apprehension than dread, and dread less than terror and fright. The force of this passion, beginning with the most moderate degree, may be thus expressed, fear, dread, terror, fright. Fear is accompanied with a desire to avoid or ward off the expected evil. Fear is an uneasiness of mind, upon the thought of future evil likely to befall us."

From Vine's Dictionary we read about fear:

"Reverential fear of God as a controlling motive of the life, in matters spiritual and moral, not a mere fear of his power and righteous retribution, but a wholesome dread of displeasing him, a fear which banishes the terror that shrinks from his presence, and which influences the disposition and attitude of one's circumstances are guided by trusting God, through the indwelling Spirit of God. The reverential fear of God will inspire constant carefulness in dealing with others in his fear."

So when we consider these definitions of fear there seems to be two main characteristics that one can apprehend from it. A fear based on filial understanding, and a type of fear based on natural or slavish comprehension. It is clear that the natural form of fear has no real value. It is also clear that the natural form of fear is heavy, overwhelming, and depressive. While the filial is defined as follows:

"Pertaining to a son or daughter; becoming a child in relation to his parents. Filial love is such an affection as a child naturally bears to his parents. Filial duty or obedience is such duty or obedience as the child owes to his parents."

> *For all who are led by the Spirit of God are sons of God. For you did not receive the spirit of slavery to fall back into fear, but you have received the Spirit of adoption as sons, by whom we cry, "Abba! Father!" The Spirit himself bears witness with our spirit that we are children of God."*
>
> *Romans 8:14-16*

This being said, it is vitally important for us to realize that once we are saved, we are now purchased by the blood of Jesus and made sons and daughters of God. We have now moved from a former, natural fear of judgment into a *"filial"* pure fear of God that causes us to love him. For once we were children of the devil or children of wrath, we lived then under natural fear; whereas, now we are reconciled children of adoption, and we live under holy fear of our new Father. Setting this as an example, let us ponder what happens to people who do not dwell in the true fear of their father. Let us look at a sad passage of scripture in Isaiah.

> *For the LORD has poured out upon you a spirit of deep sleep, and has closed your eyes (the prophets), and covered your heads (the seers). And the vision of all this has become to you like the words of a book that is sealed. When men give it to one who can read, saying, "Read this," he says, "I cannot, for it is sealed." And when they give the book to one who cannot read, saying, "Read this," he says, "I cannot read." And the Lord said: "Because this people draw near with their mouth and honor me with their lips, while their hearts are far from me, and their fear of me is a commandment taught by men.*
>
> *Isaiah 29:10-13*

When we read these verses truly they are a great sadness. Let's look at this last phrase deeper. "...and their fear of me is a commandment taught by men..." The Lord had several complaints against the people, and the wrong fear of the Lord was one of them. So because they walked away from the fear of the Lord, and his heart, he put blinders on them. What do you suppose the Father's heart feels at this point? Clearly he is not happy but sad, that men are speaking on their own behalf, trying to force people to fear Him. If we do anything in life driven by tradition, commandment, or opinions that are other than the heart of the Father, we are in danger of manipulated fear. Interestingly enough how often do we do things, out of the fear of man, rather than the true fear of God? The fear of man produces un-pure motives, and empty results. While the fear of Lord produces life, and teaches you that you are a son, not an enemy. At this point, strivings tend to cease. Only God can teach our hearts to fear Him in the correct manner. It is by seeing Him in his glory, by seeing him in his righteousness, by seeing him in Holy Awe that will produce a legitimate heart of holy fear towards the Lord.

Real fear of the Lord does not leave anyone standing. At the name of Jesus every knee shall bow; that, bowing before the Lord is reverent, and holy fear of a righteous Savior. If anyone walks around in Christianity without a legitimate fear of God, his words will have no spiritual backbone whatsoever. Let the Lord God Almighty teach you personally what true fear and respect are. His food for you will cause you to never stray from his path. This is what really happens when one sees Jesus!

> *Like the appearance of the bow that is in the cloud on the day of rain, so was the appearance of the brightness all around. Such was the appearance of the likeness of the glory of the LORD. And when I saw it, I fell on my face, and I heard the voice of one speaking.*
>
> *Ezekiel 1:28*

Then I turned to see the voice that was speaking to me, and on turning I saw seven golden lampstands, and in the midst of the lampstands one like a son of man, clothed with a long robe and with a golden sash around his chest. The hairs of his head were white, like white wool, like snow. His eyes were like a flame of fire, his feet were like burnished bronze, refined in a furnace, and his voice was like the roar of many waters. In his right hand he held seven stars, from his mouth came a sharp two-edged sword, and his face was like the sun shining in full strength. When I saw him, I fell at his feet as though dead.

Revelation 1:12-17

This is true reverent, fear of God. Our society has a real void of fear for any leader. This is especially true in Western Culture. We have lived and governed our society in a way where respect and honor have vanished from and for our main leaders. Perhaps, years and millennial ago, fear for "Good Authority" was not seen in a negative light. There were many in older history who were appropriately respected in society. In our current society fearing someone is seen as negative, because ethics and morality have diminished in much of our leadership. Fear and love no longer walk together, and fear is once again demanded instead of desired. Fear in its truest form is not about terror, it is about *honoring one that deserves respect.* Once again, we fear the Lord now, because we are saved and we know that he loves us. Therefore we revere him with utmost respect and honor.

Now that we understand what real fear of the Lord is, let's take a look at several scriptures that talk about the fear of the Lord. These verses reveal God's heart behind this topic of fear, and show us the true fruit the fear of the Lord produces in us.

The fear of the LORD is clean, enduring forever; the rules of the LORD are true, and righteous altogether.
Psalms 19:9

The friendship of the LORD is for those who fear him, and he makes known to them his covenant.

Psalms 25:14

The fear of the LORD is the beginning of wisdom; all those who practice it have a good understanding. His praise endures forever!

Psalms 111:10

The fear of the LORD is the beginning of knowledge; fools despise wisdom and instruction

Proverbs 1:7

The fear of the LORD is hatred of evil. Pride and arrogance and the way of evil and perverted speech I hate.

Proverbs 8:13

In the fear of the LORD one has strong confidence, and his children will have a refuge. The fear of the LORD is a fountain of life that one may turn away from the snares of death.

Proverbs 14:26-27

By steadfast love and faithfulness iniquity is atoned for, and by the fear of the LORD one turns away from evil.

Proverbs 16:6

The fear of the LORD leads to life, and whoever has it rests satisfied; he will not be visited by harm.

Proverbs 19:23

Let not your heart envy sinners, but continue in the fear of the LORD all the day.

Proverbs 23:17

Do you not fear me? declares the LORD. Do you not tremble before me? I placed the sand as the boundary for the sea, a perpetual barrier that it cannot pass; though the waves toss, they cannot prevail; though they roar, they cannot pass over it. But this people has a stubborn and rebellious heart; they have turned aside and gone away. They do not say in their hearts, 'Let us fear the LORD our God, who gives the rain in its season, the autumn rain and the spring rain, and keeps for us the weeks appointed for the harvest.

Jeremiah 5:22-24

Once we know what God deserves, and once we know the true fear of the Lord, then we are motivated and compelled to speak. We then speak to everything that is darkness, because knowing the Father we know there is no darkness in him. As stated in Chapter 1, the Father burns for Righteousness, and there is only one way to walk in this righteousness: by the fear of the Lord. "For the fear of the Lord is to hate evil," (Proverbs 8:13). If we are communing with the Lord, then we see his righteousness, and we fear him. If you have grasped the fear of the Lord, you are starting to prepare for prophetic ministry. To close this chapter it is essential to reveal the hope in returning to the fear of the Lord for anyone who has left it, nor understood this fear correctly. It is right to fear the Lord!

> *For behold the day is coming, burning like an oven, and all the proud, all who do wickedly will be stubble. And the day which is coming shall burn them up, says the Lord of Hosts,that will leave them neither root nor branch. But to you who fear my name, the Sun of Righteousness shall rise with healing in his wings; and you shall go out and grow fat like stall-fed calves. You shall trample the wicked, for they shall be ashes under the soles of your feet, on the day that I do this, says the Lord of Hosts.*
>
> *Malachi 4:1-3*

A fearful Christian is a Fat Christian (In a good way). A Christian who fears the Lord will be fattened with his goodness, and will be joyful and not afraid of the enemy; but will triumph over opposition. A true fearful Christian is also one who rests in the perfect love of the Lord, each day and everyday. Below is the fruit of right fear.

Then those who feared the LORD spoke with one another. The LORD paid attention and heard them, and a book of remembrance was written before him of those who feared the LORD and esteemed his name. "They shall be mine, says the LORD of hosts, in the day when I make up my treasured possession, and I will spare them as a man spares his son who serves him. Then once more you shall see the distinction between the righteous and the wicked, between one who serves God and one who does not serve him.

Malachi 3:16-18

This is our victory as Christians! If we return to right fear of the Lord, then God will take back and remove the blinders and delusions that were placed there from before. If you fear the Lord and dwell on His name, then discernment will return to a people and a generation who have wandered away from Fear of the Lord. Walking your calling out as a prophet will always begin with the fear of the Lord.

Having therefore these promises, dearly beloved, let us cleanse ourselves from all filthiness of the flesh and spirit, perfecting holiness in the fear of God.

2 Corinthians 7:1

Therefore, knowing the fear of the Lord, we persuade others...

2 Corinthians 5:11a

CHAPTER THREE

The Zeal of the Lord

If you are walking in the true Fear of the Lord, His zeal will soon accompany you on your path. Zeal is not an option, or an accessory to the Christian life, it is the Holy Fuel of your inner life. As we will find out in the following definitions regarding zeal, it is not something that is lacking in true Christianity. Zeal is first of all pure, righteous, holy, and altogether unstoppable. It is the garments of a worthy bridegroom, and his passion for his bride. So let us take a look at several sources that define zeal Biblically, and extra-Biblically.

From Webster's we read about Zeal:

"Passionate ardor in the pursuit of any thing. In general, zeal is an eagerness of desire to accomplish or obtain some object, and it may be manifested either in favor of any person or thing, or in opposition to it, and in a good or bad cause."

From Easton's Bible Dictionary:

"An earnest temper may be enlightened or ignorant, and misdirected. As a Christian grace it must be directed on right principles, and directed to right ends. It is ascribed also to God."

Hebrew Wording for zeal:

"Kaw-Naw" To be zealous, to be jealous or envious, move to or provoke to jealousy.

Greek wording for zeal:

"Dzay-los" Properly stated heat, in a favorable sense Ardor, or jealousy as of a husband, indignation, fervent mind.

In this most recent definition, we are shedding light on a large portion of the word's meaning when we see that it is properly used by a husband for his wife. This sheds incredible light to us when we reveal this passion of God towards his bride. In a sense, it could be properly said, "God has a *zealous,* burning, passion for His bride to be completely his." Let's take a look at another word that reveals this covenant passion deeper, and that is the word *fidelity.*

From Webster's, we read about fidelity:

"1. Faithfulness; careful and exact observance of duty, or performance of obligations. We expect fidelity in a public minister, in an agent or trustee, in a domestic servant, in a friend. 2. Firm adherence to a person or party with which one is united, or to which one is bound; loyalty; as the fidelity of subjects to their king or government; the fidelity of a tenant or liege to his lord. 3. Observance of the marriage covenant; as the fidelity of a husband or wife. 4. Honesty; veracity; adherence to truth; as the fidelity of a witness."

So in many ways fidelity, and zeal are not very far apart from each other. When it says God is a jealous God, we have the duty to express his jealousy towards all mankind correctly. In that, he has pure, and righteous burning love for us as his bride. Many people stumble at the much coined phrase, "God is a jealous God." They have stumbled because they have placed human emotions, and definitions in place of God's Holy Character. We cannot properly understand God as a jealous God, unless we step outside of human thinking and understanding. God is creator, maker, author, and finisher of everything, he has every right to demand worship. When people are jealous, and demanding we see them as selfish, overbearing, tyrants, and we must not put God in that same category. How can we miss on this wording of Jealousy, and Zeal? We miss to understand it when we forget that it is God's love that moves him to jealously protect, and zealously redeem his bride from trouble. God demands true worship, because after all he has done for us, he deserves true worship. If you truly grasp this truth, you will do well.

The whole story and theme of the Bible is simply put, "God's journey to redeem, his bride back to Himself." Therefore when marriage or anything that represents marriage is portrayed in Scripture, God's heart is not far from it. There are so many places that talk about marriage in the Old Covenant, but there is one account that really makes clear the Zeal of The Lord to us. This is the account of Phinehas.

> *While Israel lived in Shittim, the people began to whore with the daughters of Moab. These invited the people to the sacrifices of their gods, and the people ate and bowed down to their gods. So Israel yoked himself to Baal of Peor. And the anger of the LORD was kindled against Israel. And the LORD said to Moses, "Take all the chiefs of the people and hang them in the sun before the LORD, that the fierce anger of the LORD may turn away from Israel."*

> *And Moses said to the judges of Israel, "Each of you kill those of his men who have yoked themselves to Baal of Peor." And behold, one of the people of Israel came and brought a Midianite woman to his family, in the sight of Moses and in the sight of the whole congregation of the people of*

Israel, while they were weeping in the entrance of the tent of meeting. When Phinehas the son of Eleazar, son of Aaron the priest, saw it, he rose and left the congregation and took a spear in his hand and went after the man of Israel into the chamber and pierced both of them, the man of Israel and the woman through her belly. Thus the plague on the people of Israel was stopped. Nevertheless, those who died by the plague were twenty-four thousand. And the LORD said to Moses, "Phinehas the son of Eleazar, son of Aaron the priest, has turned back my wrath from the people of Israel, in that he was jealous with my jealousy among them, so that I did not consume the people of Israel in my jealousy. Therefore say, 'Behold, I give to him my covenant of peace, and it shall be to him and to his descendants after him the covenant of a perpetual priesthood, because he was jealous for his God and made atonement for the people of Israel.'" The name of the slain man of Israel, who was killed with the Midianite woman, was Zimri the son of Salu, chief of a father's house belonging to the Simeonites. And the name of the Midianite woman who was killed was Cozbi the daughter of Zur, who was the tribal head of a father's house in Midian.

Numbers 25:1-15

And in Psalms we also read of Phinehas:

Then they yoked themselves to the Baal of Peor, and ate sacrifices offered to the dead; they provoked the LORD to anger with their deeds, and a plague broke out among them. Then Phinehas stood up and intervened, and the plague was stayed. And that was counted to him as righteousness from generation to generation forever.

Psalms 106:28-31

Looking back at the account of Phinehas more, we see the marriage breech among the children of Israel. They left their first love, God, as they disregarded his commandments; instead they cleaved unto pagan idolatry and wickedness. The children of Israel were so incredibly arrogant and defiled in this, that one brought his new "pagan wife" before the very tent of Moses. This was a true slap in the face of God's covenant to the children of Israel. This very act of arrogant betrayal initiated the anger of the Lord in response to his zealous love for the people. Looking at the heart of God here shows us his horrific pain while watching his dear children fornicate. What parent rejoices over such defiant debauchery? As one of God's appointed priests and messengers, Phinehas took the cause of the Lord seriously. In response to such an act, the zeal of the Lord manifested in Phinehas.

This account is both heart gripping and intense to read. Yet, there was a covenant given to Phinehas from the Lord because of his zeal. Hallelujah for God's zeal demonstrated to all during the Old Covenant! Phinehas did right in the eyes of the Lord. Now we are in the New Covenant, and this changes the means for demonstrating zeal, but it does not change the heart behind the zeal. If it was counted to Phinehas as righteousness then and the sinner's died, how much more will it be counted to prophetic people as righteousness now if the sinners are confronted, repent, turn from their wicked ways and live?

Truly, if you look at God's response to Phinehas you see his heart filled with true zeal. Yet don't think for one minute that God wants anyone to die, because he doesn't. Let's once again remind ourselves of two verses before we move on.

> *Have I any pleasure in the death of the wicked, declares the Lord GOD, and not rather that he should turn from his way and live?*
> *Ezekiel 18:23*

> *The Lord is not slow to fulfill his promise as some count slowness, but is patient toward you, not wishing that any should perish, but that all should reach repentance.*
> *2 Peter 3:9*

Zeal = Jealousy which turns into Urgency, which turns into Extreme Action, which in part turns into accomplishment. Looking at Phinehas we see this very formula happen. God's heart was made visible in regards to sin, this debauchery was seen, and Phinehas went into immediate action. He did not let the grass grow under his feet with being obedient to the Lord. Even though the extreme measure of this account was death in the Old Covenant, the accomplishment was victory. Since the Old Covenant is a type and shadow of the New Covenant, the victory now is repentance. However the only thing that doesn't change in the New Covenant is the pressing heart of God about sin. God's heart has not changed and his urgency for sin to be dealt with has not changed either. Therefore when sin is noticed, urgency is greatly required. Every moment sin is in the camp, or temple the Holy Spirit urges us to deal with it immediately.

The Lord responds to sin, idolatry, rebellion, and captivity with zeal. Concerning the zeal of the Lord there is an essence of passion, urgency, and fiery forth going, with complete authority. Zeal has to do with fidelity and jealousy. Transgression fuels the zeal to action.

Now that we have taken a look at the example of Phinehas who had the zeal of the Lord, let's take a closer look at what the Lord himself does with zeal. The end result of the Lord's zeal, was putting Jesus to death on the cross for the sins of all. God's righteous zeal was satisfied when the blood of Jesus was spilled on Calvary.

> *For to us a child is born, to us a son is given; and the government shall be upon his shoulder, and his name shall be called Wonderful Counselor, Mighty God, Everlasting Father, Prince of Peace. Of the increase of his government and of peace there will be no end, on the throne of David and over his kingdom, to establish it and to uphold it with justice and with righteousness from this time forth and forevermore. The zeal of the LORD of hosts will do this.*
>
> *Isaiah 9:6-7*

Father God had a purpose and mission for Jesus to complete. Therefore God sent Jesus to fulfill that purpose of redemption. The bottom line is this: when God sets in his heart to do something it will surely be accomplished. After the fall of man, God in the forefront of his heart desired to redeem and restore his people back to him, and give his son a pure and spotless bride. He became jealous and zealous for the heart of his people to return. In essence he is saying, "If any other thing grips the heart of my people I will go to drastic measures and extreme actions to bring them back to me." The zeal of the Lord for the redemption of his people would surely be accomplished no matter what.

What is often difficult for all of us to understand, is the fact that the Lord basically has two forms of Zeal. On one hand zeal is motivated because of sin and transgression. On the other hand there is a kind of zeal fueled by love for redemption and reconciliation. Both demanded satisfaction because of who God is, and what God said about sin. The problem is, humanity is guilty of sin, and unrighteousness. So the question is, "How does God satisfy his zeal of wrath and his zeal of passion together?" The answer is Jesus! God's zeal was so great that he sent his only son into the world to become a man, bear man's sin and take the wrath of God upon himself, while dying on a cross to win humanity back to him. By sending his own son he proved, he would stop at nothing to save and redeem a fallen people.

God gave Jesus the task to go to earth, and redeem this fallen race. Jesus took on the cloak of Zeal, in obedience and honor to the Father God. Zeal in its truest form will take you to extremes, but the end product will always be redemption and restoration.

Look at the end result of God's zeal for his people: God forsook God for mankind, even to the point of Jesus taking the place of the sinner, being treated as a sinner, and being punished by his father for their sins. Jesus the eternal God actually died for you and me because of God's zeal to have back his children. When Jesus died on the cross he satisfied the zeal of wrath, so that the zeal of passion would be fulfilled. For those who choose Christ Jesus, the wrath of God is no longer over them. When they choose

Jesus they now have unhindered fellowship with God. The end result of God's extreme Zeal towards us is redeemed fellowship.

Once Jesus died on the cross he returned back to the Father to send us the Holy Spirit. The Holy Spirit came with gifts in hand to distribute as he so desired. Some may have larger portions of zeal, while others smaller. Regardless, every gift from the Lord will be dipped in zeal. Christians stand for truth, and this is motivated by correct zeal. Zeal is the Holy fuel which motivates us to walk circumspectly to the world's system. However to properly teach and exhort I must warn us and speak of the zeal used without the Holy Spirit. Let's briefly look at two New Testament examples of men with zeal, who stepped out of place.

> *Then Simon Peter, having a sword, drew it and struck the high priest's servant and cut off his right ear. (The servant's name was Malchus.) So Jesus said to Peter, "Put your sword into its sheath; shall I not drink the cup that the Father has given me?*

> *John 18:10-11*

Having a full heart to rescue Jesus, and function correctly for the Lord, Peter took the mission into a natural realm and stepped out of the Spirit realm. By doing this, Peter actually momentarily got in the way of the true mission of Jesus. Yet, God worked it all out to the good, and healed the man's ear. Never can we take Christianity into our hands in this way now. We are now in the New Covenant. It is no longer a slash and burn ministry, but a sew and heal ministry. If you cannot accept this message as a prophet, you will be a loose cannon in the body of Christ. You can have zeal all day long for the Lord, but unless your eyes see the big picture of redemption, you will only bring destruction and derailment. Take warning.

Another case of improper zealous behavior is the case of Saul the Pharisee. Let's take a look at what he did in his original zeal.

> *Then they cast him out of the city and stoned him.*

And the witnesses laid down their garments at the feet of a young man named Saul. And as they were stoning Stephen, he called out, "Lord Jesus, receive my spirit." And falling to his knees he cried out with a loud voice, "Lord, do not hold this sin against them." And when he had said this, he fell asleep. And Saul approved of his execution. And there arose on that day a great persecution against the church in Jerusalem, and they were all scattered throughout the regions of Judea and Samaria, except the apostles. Devout men buried Stephen and made great lamentation over him. But Saul was ravaging the church, and entering house after house, he dragged off men and women and committed them to prison.

Acts 7:58-8:3

Then as we know it Saul was converted radically, and became a Spirit filled, zealous believer for the Lord Jesus. Even later Paul himself acknowledges his wrong usage of zeal.

Though I myself have reason for confidence in the flesh also. If anyone else thinks he has reason for confidence in the flesh, I have more: circumcised on the eighth day, of the people of Israel, of the tribe of Benjamin, a Hebrew of Hebrews; as to the law, a Pharisee; as to zeal, a persecutor of the church; as to righteousness under the law, blameless. But whatever gain I had, I counted as loss for the sake of Christ.

Philippians 3:4-7

Brothers, my heart's desire and prayer to God for them is that they may be saved. For I bear them witness that they have a zeal for God, but not according to knowledge.

Romans 10:1-2

Paul using his testimony and wisdom showed what zeal can do without proper knowledge and the leading of the Spirit. Both Paul and Peter had zeal, and yet both needed to learn its proper place. When each of us get saved, filled with Spirit, and follow the Lord, it is easy to walk, if not run in religious zeal at the beginning of your prophetic journey. But the victory and triumph comes when your zeal is bridled and tempered correctly in the classroom of the Lord. The Lord will not let you out to minister until you have learned stability and control.

Zeal must always go forth in the knowledge and character of God. As Paul stated, the Pharisee's had zeal without proper knowledge. This is why we as prophets must have the testimony of Jesus, "which is the Spirit of Prophecy".

If the testimony of Jesus is not present in your heart and spirit, it will lead you to become a legalistic Pharisee. As a legalistic Pharisee you may find yourself persecuting the church, instead of restoring it.

The prophet must know what he is zealous for, in order to carry out his actions rightly. If you as a prophet stay cross centered with your ear to the heartbeat of the Father, then and only then, will your zeal produce fruit in due season. Let God, know you, and teach you Himself, and then you can hear his heart.

As it has been stated there is a burning passion in God's zeal for righteousness. We must burn with that same unction. Zeal begins with self-examination in light of Jesus. Zeal will cause us to address what is in our own hearts that is in opposition to God. Once the beam is removed from our own life, we can address the things that go against God, in the lives of others. None of us are perfect vessels, but one would do well to not be a hypocrite when addressing the sins of others. If you are struggling in a particular sin and do not have current victory, it may do you well to wait to address it in someone else. But if you are walking correctly, the zeal of the Lord in our lives will compel us to speak even when we do not wish to. We must be jealous for God to be glorified at all costs.

My goal is to see you walk in your prophetic calling correctly. If you have zeal, then you must see God correctly. If you do not see and know God correctly it is not too late to fix that. My prayer is that you will honestly examine the zeal that you think you have. If redemption and restoration are in your mind for the glory of Jesus, you have correct Zeal. If you burn with a passion against sin and debauchery, yet desire to see the lost saved from it, you have correct zeal. One of the best ways to monitor your zeal, is to listen for redemption in your speech. Ask God to speak to you, and reveal your true heart. True zeal is not what your works brings to God's kingdom, it's what God's Kingdom brings to your works. This zeal always starts with God, will always point to God, and will always listen to God. Let the zeal of the Lord fuel you for the sake of redemption. If you are clothed in the garment of zeal, your ministry will always produce life, not death.

> *So the angel who spoke with me said to me, "Proclaim, saying, 'Thus says the LORD of hosts:"I am zealous for Jerusalem And for Zion with great zeal."*

> *Zechariah 1:14 (NKJV)*

CHAPTER FOUR

The Prophetic Sigh

Whether you grew up in a church family, or you were saved from a non-religious affiliation, something changes when you taste the Lord. How does the world taste to you currently? What consumes your mind daily? Are your thoughts of the kingdom of Heaven or the kingdom of earth? Are you currently thinking of all the new gadgets and technology? Have you subscribed to materialism, and the ways of man? Are you entrenched in the ways of the world or are you made weary from the darkness you see? Do you find yourself praying at people or for people? When you walk down busy streets is your Spirit content, or distressed? Is the earth a hotel stop over for you, or have you called it home? Has sin and debauchery grieved you to the point of despair or anguish? Do you find yourself begging and pleading to the Lord to change and redeem these situations? If you can answer the above questions correctly, and if you have and are experiencing the deep pains like the grief above, then you are clearly walking with *"The Prophetic Sigh"*!

Here is a modern definition for the word Sigh (From Webster's):

"A single deep respiration; a long breath; the inhaling of larger quantity of air than usual, and the sudden emission of it. This is an effort of nature to dilate the lungs and give vigor to the circulation of the blood, when the action of the heart and arteries is languid from grief, depression of spirits, weakness or want of exercise. Hence sighs are indications of grief of debility."

We all sigh for different reasons in life. Some are over things that mean nothing, and are worthless. For example a child who cries or sighs when he has lost his toy. Another example is of someone who spent so much money on lottery tickets, and did not win the lottery, or the person who did not get good seats for a rock show, or a person who got off work 15 minutes late and missed his television show. There are many sighs that stem from disappointments from not obtaining fleshly desires. The sigh we will be talking about in this chapter is the sigh that originates in the heart of God.

As it has been stated in other chapters the father burns for righteousness and for redemption. When his children go against him and do not listen to his will for their lives, this causes God to grieve and sigh. God is not a dictator, and wants mankind to choose his ways without being forced. For true love to be manifest, there must be a free will choice of that love. God is waiting for a response!

The scripture paints a very clear picture of how God longs and sighs for the human race. Let's take a look at a few examples of his heart cry for us.

Is Ephraim my dear son? Is he my darling child? For as often as I speak against him, I do remember him still. Therefore my heart yearns for him; I will surely have mercy on him, declares the LORD.

Jeremiah 31:20

Therefore I will judge you, O house of Israel, every one according to his ways, declares the Lord GOD. Repent and turn from all your transgressions, lest iniquity be your ruin. Cast away from you all the transgressions that you have committed, and make yourselves a new heart and a new spirit! Why will you die, O house of Israel? For I have no pleasure in the death of anyone, declares the Lord GOD; so turn, and live.

Ezekiel 18:30-32

These are just two of many places in the Old Covenant that reveal the heart of the Father towards all of us. The sins of the people required judgment, yet the heart of the Father desires mercy and salvation. Here he is talking about the sins of Ephraim, knowing they deserve judgment; yet, his heart yearns for them to be spared. In the second verse we are again reminded that the Father does not delight in the death of anyone. Many people think God is a mean God and sends sinners to hell without caring. But, the truest heart of the Father was that no one be lost. For hell was not created for man, but for the devil and the fallen angels. God sighs for all of mankind, to live and be redeemed. His sigh is pure, not hostile. "Then he will say to those on his left, 'Depart from me, you cursed, into the eternal fire prepared for the devil and his angels...'" (Matthew 25:41).

As a side note before we move on: Do not be afraid to speak about hell to lost people, but always have in mind this verse, because it is the Father's desire that none should perish. Though some arrogant people, must be confronted with such a sharp word that it shocks them to the reality of their state or current condition and motivates them to change direction. Regardless, the Father does sigh for everyone to be redeemed from the fires of hell. This is why he sent his son Jesus to carry this sigh on his behalf. So looking now at Jesus we will see the same heart of the Father, come to us in human flesh.

Once again, we will look to Jesus to hear from the Father. Jesus faithfully portrayed the Father's heart for us as an invitation for eternal freedom and life.

Jesus the Lamb of God was sent to the earth to redeem us as our ransom. He left heaven, an immaculately perfect place, that does not know darkness or shifting shadows whatsoever. He left a state of utter perfection, to commit himself to the task of redeeming a fallen people. He put on human flesh and human emotions to carry out this mission. He was born, lived, and walked on this earth for 33 years. He has seen, heard, and witnessed the wretchedness of mankind. If there was anyone who could say they had a sigh over the state of man, it was Jesus.

While he walked with challenging disciples, ate among sinners, and was ridiculed by the religious arena, his sigh grew even deeper. His end result was the Father's completed will for his life, even to the point of death on a cross. The very people who rejected him were among those hard hearts for whom he came to die. After speaking at length against the hypocrisy and sins of the religious leaders, you still hear his heart come out at the end. Let's take a look.

Matthew 23:13-30 *(all verses paraphrased into these few sentences)* "Woe to you, blind guides, Woe to you Scribes and Pharisees, you blind guides, you hypocrites." Perhaps the Message best summarizes the heart of this passage with these words: "I've had it with you! You're hopeless, you religion scholars, you Pharisees! Frauds! Your lives are roadblocks to God's kingdom. You refuse to enter, and won't let anyone else in either..." (Matt. 23:13).

Yet in verse 37 we see the heart of Jesus, which revealed the heart of the Father.

> *O Jerusalem, Jerusalem, the city that kills the prophets and stones those who are sent to it! How often would I have gathered your children together as a hen gathers her brood under her wings, and you were not willing!*
> *Matthew 23:37*

If they would have let Jesus hold them, he would have reached over and held those Pharisees! Yet their hardened hearts rejected him, causing him to grieve and sigh on their behalf. After Jesus died, rose from the grave, and returned to heaven, he then sent us the Holy Spirit to continue his mission. The Holy Spirit now carries the sigh back to the Father on our behalf, even when we don't realize it. So as a recap, the sigh started with the Father, was passed on to Jesus, then was given to the Holy Spirit. Now that the Holy Spirit is on task with us after Pentecost, we hear the sigh each day communicated to us by the Spirit. Sometimes we know it in our heart, and sometimes only the Spirit knows what he is praying for.

> *Likewise the Spirit helps us in our weakness. For we do not know what to pray for as we ought, but the Spirit himself intercedes for us with groanings too deep for words. And he who searches hearts knows what is the mind of the Spirit, because the Spirit intercedes for the saints according to the will of God.*
>
> Romans 8:26-27

The Holy Spirit received the sigh for man and in return wishes to communicate to our hearts this same burden. The Bottom line is, when the *"Prophetic Sigh"* comes to man, we are just being asked to join it, not originate it. There are both Old Testament accounts as well as New Testament accounts of the Spirit of the Lord coming to man with this burden. Because the Lord is looking for people who are true to him, and will answer to His call for redemption. Here are a few places that we can look at this exchange.

> *And the LORD said unto him, Go through the midst of the city, through the midst of Jerusalem, and set a mark upon the foreheads of the men that sigh and that cry for all the abominations that be done in the midst thereof.*
>
> *Ezekiel 9:4 (KJV)*

Sigh therefore, thou son of man, with the breaking of thy loins; and with bitterness sigh before their eyes. And it shall be, when they say unto thee, Wherefore sighest thou? that thou shalt answer, For the tidings; because it cometh: and every heart shall melt, and all hands shall be feeble, and every spirit shall faint, and all knees shall be weak as water: behold, it cometh, and shall be brought to pass, saith the Lord GOD.

Ezekiel 21:6-7 (KJV)

Whether God is looking for those who already sigh, or he is commanding the prophet to sigh, God wants the exact same burden that he has. If you are willing to hear the heart of the Lord, you will receive it. If you are not willing to hear his sigh, chances are you will miss it. As Jesus demonstrated, he showed us that He wanted the Fathers heart and will to be done. This is the true sigh of any called minister of God.

Another great example of *"Prophetic Sigh"* is found in the life of Isaiah, who truly sheds light to us in this matter. For the purpose of this chapter it is exceedingly helpful for you to see this point made clear in the life of Isaiah. Therefore it will be important for you to stop and read the first 5 chapters before continuing on in this chapter here. Let's resume after you have read Isaiah Chapters 1-5.

Isaiah is walking prophetically in his life during the first five chapters. This burden he has is growing and grew with an incredible intensity towards the people.

Then in chapter 5, we see the message again of *"Woe"* come out towards the people. It's clear judgment and destruction are necessary and are being pronounced over the people. Isaiah is seeing correctly in many ways, yet the rubber hits the road in chapter 6.

In the year that King Uzziah died I saw the Lord sitting upon a throne, high and lifted up; and the train of his robe filled the temple. Above him stood the seraphim. Each had six wings: with two he covered his face, and with two he covered his feet, and with two he flew. And one called to another and said: "Holy, holy, holy is the LORD of hosts; the whole earth is full of his glory!"

And the foundations of the thresholds shook at the voice of him who called, and the house was filled with smoke. And I said: "Woe is me! For I am lost; for I am a man of unclean lips, and I dwell in the midst of a people of unclean lips; for my eyes have seen the King, the LORD of hosts!" Then one of the seraphim flew to me, having in his hand a burning coal that he had taken with tongs from the altar.

And he touched my mouth and said: "Behold, this has touched your lips; your guilt is taken away, and your sin atoned for." And I heard the voice of the Lord saying, "Whom shall I send, and who will go for us?" Then I said, "Here I am! Send me.

Isaiah 6:1-8

These verses speak for themselves in many ways. But in my honest opinion I feel this is where his real ministry and sigh begins. The final woe came upon Isaiah himself, after he saw the Lord in his glory. This is where our first *"Prophetic Sigh"* must begin. We need to see the Glory of God! When Isaiah saw the Glory of God, he knew he was not even worthy enough to worship God. At that point what an awesome privilege Isaiah had to see his own wretchedness. The mercy of the Lord brought the coal to his mouth, because God desired to use that mouth for his purposes. God also desires to use your mouth prophetically for his purposes, but you need that coal also. Jesus' blood is our New Covenant Coal for our mouth, and entire body. This is the new way to purify us in light of the New Covenant. We are as much now in need of this as Isaiah was back then. When we are purified by the Coals of Jesus, we are then made ready for battle. So now when God asks, "Whom shall I send?" We can say, "Here I am, send me!" If you have not correctly looked first at yourself in light of the Lord, you will not be able to see and discern others correctly. God's sigh, is purified by God's fire.

In conclusion, you cannot share and partake of the Sigh of the Lord, if you are sharing and partaking of the things of this world. Slowly but surely, you will come to know that you cannot relate with the children of darkness. You will also come to know that you cannot relate with many people who call themselves Christians. However you will not isolate nor remove yourself from the world and become a monk. You must know God, speak his words, share his burden, and declare his truth. To do this, you must remain in this world as a candle burning bright for him. His sigh begins in you when you come to the end of yourself like Isaiah did. As this desire comes, be ready and willing like Isaiah to go on behalf of the Lord, no matter what the situation is ahead of you.

When you get His true burden of sigh, carry it as long as you live. One day we will have a release of that Prophetic Sigh, and on that day all *"Sighing"* will be complete and finished! Let's read where it ends:

> *And the ransomed of the LORD shall return, and come to Zion with songs and everlasting joy upon their heads: they shall obtain joy and gladness, and sorrow and sighing shall flee away.*

> *Isaiah 35:10*

These above mentioned sighs can be speaking about earthly things, pain, or from other grievances caused by living on this dark earth. But for the Prophet his sigh will be over and complete. All will be made right! We will see and have Jesus completely! "But according to his promise we are waiting for new heavens and a new earth in which righteousness dwells,"(2 Peter 3:13). Until this happens we carry the sigh, and preach the righteousness of God!

In writing this book, my deep prophetic sigh is, that you will be equipped correctly, and serve the Lord faithfully. Ask God today for his true "Prophetic Sigh".

CHAPTER 5

God's Authority and Order

In a society and world spinning away from values and morals, the topic of authority and order will no doubt be offensive to many people. It is my plain and simple task in this chapter to briefly visit this vital topic for the health of our ministry. I wish to make it clear before this chapter begins that I am not painting authority from God as legalistic.

In fact, being under authority is quite freeing in my honest opinion. I am also not attempting to fully explain the authority and relationship of the Holy Trinity in this chapter, though they provide the only perfect example for us to both observe and follow. To say it clear and simply, I wish to convey in this chapter there are many God ordained circles of authority God has placed in each of our lives. And by doing this I wish to encourage all of us to walk under authority. If you cannot walk under authority in a church, job, or society then you are in danger of a failed ministry. It is my prayer that we all recognize God's authority and order in His kingdom work, and furthermore in each of our lives.

Authority as defined by Webster's:

"The power derived from opinion, respect or esteem; influence of character or office; credit; as the authority of age or example, which is submitted to or respected, in some measure, as a law, or rule of action. That which is claimed in justification or support of opinions and measures. Weight of testimony; credibility. Weight of character; respectability; dignity. Legal power, or a right to command or to act."

Submit as defined by Vine's & Webster's:

"To retire, withdraw and to yield. To yield, resign or surrender to the power, will or authority of another. To be submissive; to yield without murmuring."

Subject as defined by Vine's & Webster's:

"Primarily a military term, to rank under, to obey, be under obedience, held in and bound by. Being under the power and dominion of another, Placed or situate under."

A quote from Myer Pearlman, "Order is the first law of Heaven." When God created the heavens and the earth in all his authority he put everything in exact place. Secular scientists will lead to you believe that the earth, and universe are in chaotic form. However, quite on the contrary God has placed each of the stars, comets, nebulas, in their exact rightful place. Nothing is in chaos from the order of God's Kingdom. His good authority, has proven to us, you cannot separate Authority and Perfect Order. If authority, law, and order are not present then chaos reigns. So everything that Jesus did on earth was in correct order, and under the authority of the Father.

After Jesus died and sent us the Holy Spirit, the Holy Spirit functioned in correct order under the authority of Jesus and the Father. And now we as believers must function in correct order by the leading and guiding of the Holy Spirit. God is the original authority, and we must submit to Him. This is why we see the bulk of the New Testament revealing true authority, and true order. Here are some verses in scripture that reveal the authority and order at work in the Trinity Godhead. First, here are some examples of Jesus under Authority.

> *So Jesus answered them My teaching is not mine, but his who sent me. If anyone's will is to do God's will, he will know whether the teaching is from God or whether I am speaking on my own authority.*
>
> *John 7:16-17*

> *The Lord GOD has opened my ear, and I was not rebellious; I turned not backward. I gave my back to those who strike, and my cheeks to those who pull out the beard; I hid not my face from disgrace and spitting.*
>
> *Isaiah 50:5-6*

> *When Jesus had spoken these words, he lifted up his eyes to heaven, and said, "Father, the hour has come; glorify your Son that the Son may glorify you, since you have given him authority over all flesh, to give eternal life to all whom you have given him.*
>
> *John 17:1-2*

> *"I can do nothing on my own. As I hear, I judge, and my judgment is just, because I seek not my own will but the will of him who sent me."*
>
> *John 5:30*

In all his ways, Jesus walked depending, leaning and trusting upon the Father's will and authority. Jesus demonstrated to us true submissiveness, and being subject to the Father's plans, even unto death. Jesus' obedience led him to sacrifice. So when Jesus went back to heaven, he then sent us the Holy Spirit who came to us under authority.

But the Helper, the Holy Spirit, whom the Father will send in my name, he will teach you all things and bring to your remembrance all that I have said to you.

John 14:26

But when the Helper comes, whom I will send to you from the Father, the Spirit of truth, who proceeds from the Father, he will bear witness about me.

John 15:26

Nevertheless, I tell you the truth: it is to your advantage that I go away, for if I do not go away, the Helper will not come to you. But if I go, I will send him to you. And when he comes, he will convict the world concerning sin and righteousness and judgment:

John 16:7-8

When the Spirit of truth comes, he will guide you into all the truth, for he will not speak on his own authority, but whatever he hears he will speak, and he will declare to you the things that are to come. He will glorify me, for he will take what is mine and declare it to you. All that the Father has is mine; therefore I said that he will take what is mine and declare it to you.

John 16:13-15

From the beginning there has been a total unity in the Trinity. Each beautifully walks in perfect authority and order with one another. Though there are 3 persons, there is only one God. God had order in mind for building his church. The foundation and cornerstone is Jesus Christ; from the foundation of Christ the entire church is built. Disciples and apostles build upon the foundation Christ laid. When the Holy Spirit was dispersed initially at Pentecost, the gifts of the Spirit began to flow, but not without order. As the New Covenant began to reveal God's intended shape for the church, the apostles followed the direction of the Spirit to set forth its proper order. It is from this order that many of the epistles reveal proper prophetic function as stated in the Five Fold Ministry.

As a side note, you will do well to note that there are many in the body of Christ that do not recognize these applications of prophetic ministry in the current culture of Christianity. I am not part of that camp, and I don't agree and accept this way of thinking. I agree and confirm the full word of God, and what the Bible teaches about prophetic ministry in its truest form, as stated by Scripture.

Scripture that reveals prophetic order include the following passages:

Now you are the body of Christ and individually members of it. And God has appointed in the church first apostles, second prophets, third teachers, then miracles, then gifts of healing, helping, administrating, and various kinds of tongues.

1 Corinthians 12:27–28

Pursue love, and earnestly desire the spiritual gifts, especially that you may prophesy. For one who speaks in a tongue speaks not to men but to God; for no one understands him, but he utters mysteries in the Spirit.

On the other hand, the one who prophesies speaks to people for their upbuilding and encouragement and consolation. The one who speaks in a tongue builds up himself, but the one who prophesies builds up the church. Now I want you all to speak in tongues, but even more to prophesy. The one who prophesies is greater than the one who speaks in tongues, unless someone interprets, so that the church may be built up.

1 Corinthians 14:1-4

Let two or three prophets speak, and let the others weigh what is said. If a revelation is made to another sitting there, let the first be silent. For you can all prophesy one by one, so that all may learn and all be encouraged, and the spirits of prophets are subject to prophets.

1 Corinthians 14:29-32

If anyone thinks that he is a prophet, or spiritual, he should acknowledge that the things I am writing to you are a command of the Lord.

1 Corinthians 14:37

These are just a few examples from Paul about how the church should function properly and in order. Now many would disagree and say this was for the church of Corinth, because they had no order, and it is not applicable for today's church. Again I do not agree. I think we should not make it a practice to pick and choose scriptures from the New Testament that are considered "Cultural" applications only. Once you start down the road of slicing and dicing up the New Testament it turns into a subjective opinion about the use of Scripture, instead of an Authoritative word from

God. Paul in the context of the above verses, was more intently talking about order in the church gathering, including the proper place of men and women. I am not discussing that hot topic in this chapter either. Let's remain focused on prophetic order, and authority in the body of Christ. God's word is all Authority!

It will be helpful for you as a prophetic individual to know what type of church gathering you are a part of. There are many churches that do not even recognize the gifts of the Spirit in current ministry. There are other churches who do accept the ministry of the Spirit, but lawlessness is at work among them. Even still, there are other churches who welcome the ministry of the Spirit, and operate around the verses that Paul gives us in 1 Corinthians. Whatever the scenario is, it will be helpful to know what type of church you are walking in. By all means I encourage and endorse the opportunity of the "Prophetic Word" in church gatherings. Whether your prophetic word is for the body, or about the future, scripture does not lie about this topic at all, nor is it misleading. In fact once again do we hear Paul exhort another body of believers about the movements of the Holy Spirit:

> *Do not quench the Spirit. Do not despise prophecies,*
> *but test everything; hold fast what is good.*
>
> *1 Thessalonians 5:19-21*

If these proper safe guards are in place then prophetic ministry can flow correctly. Having right leaders weigh the words spoken, and test them, is a proper command of scripture. Though again let me state, that true prophetic ministry is out of sorts in the body of Christ. There are many abuses of it including lawlessness and the quenching of the Spirit. Now I could spend hours illustrating the horrible breakdown of the gifts of the Spirit, but we simply cannot here. Later in this chapter we will discuss the church scene more clearly. But for now, let us remember and focus clearly on what the point is. The point of this first section is to reveal the authority and order that God has in place in the Trinity, and in the church. Everything outside of that perfect order is chaos, and lawlessness. The ministry of prophecy in churches, must flow in proper order and authority.

If you do not have proper order in your gathering, then find a place where you will function correctly in the Body of Christ. You have a purpose in the Body!

Finding a good church is hard. Our society is filled with thousands of churches who have no real spiritual backbone. You could search your whole life for the right church. The reality is, there is no perfect church congregation. We have to bear with one another, and strive for unity in the Spirit. Though clearly there are some churches where you should walk out of and never return. In the mean time this next section's goal is to reveal good and bad examples of authority, and how you should respond in those situations. Through scripture and testimonies from my own journey, we can all learn from these following examples.

Good Example: "Jesus & the Centurion"

When he had entered Capernaum, a centurion came forward to him, appealing to him, "Lord, my servant is lying paralyzed at home, suffering terribly." And he said to him, "I will come and heal him." But the centurion replied, "Lord, I am not worthy to have you come under my roof, but only say the word, and my servant will be healed. For I too am a man under authority, with soldiers under me. And I say to one, 'Go,' and he goes, and to another, 'Come,' and he comes, and to my servant, 'Do this,' and he does it." When Jesus heard this, he marveled and said to those who followed him, "Truly, I tell you, with no one in Israel have I found such faith. I tell you, many will come from east and west and recline at table with Abraham, Isaac, and Jacob in the kingdom of heaven, while the sons of the kingdom will be thrown into the outer darkness. In that place there will be weeping and gnashing of teeth." And to the centurion Jesus said, "Go; let it be done for you as you have believed." And the servant was healed at that very moment.

Matthew 8:5-13

It is clear to see by reading the above that both the Centurion and Jesus were under correct authority. They were also both in places of authority. Each one recognized the leadership in each other, and because of this honor and respect came forth. This true miracle happened in the recognition of authority. This is one of the best examples we can see in the New Testament about authority and order. Though, there are other instances in scripture where the authority is corrupt. The following example is one of those.

Bad Example: "Samuel & Eli"

For this child I prayed, and the LORD has granted me my petition that I made to him. Therefore I have lent him to the LORD. As long as he lives, he is lent to the LORD." And he worshiped the LORD there.

1 Samuel 1:27-28

Now the sons of Eli were worthless men. They did not know the LORD. (Vs. 17) Thus the sin of the young men was very great in the sight of the LORD, for the men treated the offering of the LORD with contempt.

1 Samuel 2:12,17

Samuel was ministering before the LORD, a boy clothed with a linen ephod. And his mother used to make for him a little robe and take it to him each year when she went up with her husband to offer the yearly sacrifice.

1 Samuel 2:18-19

Now the boy Samuel was ministering to the LORD in the presence of Eli. And the word of the LORD was rare in those days; there was no frequent vision. At that time Eli, whose eyesight had begun to grow dim so that he could not see, was lying down in his own place. The lamp of God had not yet gone out, and Samuel was lying down in the temple of the LORD, where the ark of God was. Then the LORD called Samuel, and he said, "Here I am!" and ran to Eli and said, "Here I am, for you called me." But he said, "I did not call; lie down again." So he went and lay down. And the LORD called again, "Samuel!" and Samuel arose and went to Eli and said, "Here I am, for you called me." But he said, "I did not call, my son; lie down again." Now Samuel did not yet know the LORD, and the word of the LORD had not yet been revealed to him. And the LORD called Samuel again the third time. And he arose and went to Eli and said, "Here I am, for you called me." Then Eli perceived that the LORD was calling the boy. Therefore Eli said to Samuel, "Go, lie down, and if he calls you, you shall say, 'Speak, LORD, for your servant hears.'" So Samuel went and lay down in his place. And the LORD came and stood, calling as at other times, "Samuel! Samuel!" And Samuel said, "Speak, for your servant hears.

1 Samuel 3:1-10

Samuel had special training under Eli, and learned the ways of Priesthood from him in his presence. As we can see throughout these passages Samuel was very obedient and submissive to his teacher Eli. However things were about to transition for Samuel, in regards to the authority over him.

Then the LORD said to Samuel, "Behold, I am about to do a thing in Israel at which the two ears of everyone who hears it will tingle. On that day I will fulfill against Eli all that I have spoken concerning his house, from beginning to end. And I declare to him that I am about to punish his house forever, for the iniquity that he knew, because his sons were blaspheming God, and he did not restrain them. Therefore I swear to the house of Eli that the iniquity of Eli's house shall not be atoned for by sacrifice or offering forever." Samuel lay until morning; then he opened the doors of the house of the LORD. And Samuel was afraid to tell the vision to Eli. But Eli called Samuel and said, "Samuel, my son."

And he said, "Here I am." And Eli said, "What was it that he told you? Do not hide it from me. May God do so to you and more also if you hide anything from me of all that he told you." So Samuel told him everything and hid nothing from him. And he said, "It is the LORD. Let him do what seems good to him.

1 Samuel 3:11-18

Can you imagine the fear Samuel felt when he heard this massive word of judgment from the Lord against the very one who taught him? Yet even still when asked to speak from his teacher, he was obedient and walked under authority. Samuel was walking under double authority; the authority of the Lord and the authority of his mentor. Not long later we would see the judgment come forth on Eli and his household, while Samuel grew into his larger prophetic calling. Even though Samuel had to serve under a bad example of leadership, God still worked the whole situation to "The Good". Just as Samuel learned so can we, if we keep our hearts set on hearing the Lord correctly. Now let's move on to some illustrations of Good and Bad Moments of Authority and Order.

A Good Example: "Zach the Paralyzed Elder & His Wife"

As a young growing Christian I had the chance to serve in various missionary seasons of my life. In this one location I worked as a farm hand for a Jewish Christian Community which also had Hutterites living there. (For those of you who do not know what a Hutterite is, it's basically the same thing as an Amish, or Mennonite person). I worked as a farm hand for this location, and my boss was one of the three elders. His name was Zach and he was paralyzed from the waist down, from being electrocuted on a missionary journey in Africa.

Everywhere I worked, Zach went with me and was my foreman. He was a very loving man, and his wife took good care of him. Winters were tough for Zach because of his body. Though even worse for his wife, Wilma who had a skin condition on her hands and body. Her skin would get so dry that she would bleed often, and peel. Having an amazing love for his wife, Zach would wheel himself over to the sink and wash all of the dishes reaching up into the sink from his low chair. Here it is a man who is notably the male leader in his house, paralyzed and stuck in a chair reaching up to a high sink to spare his wife's hands. This was a great example of authority, stepping forward to think of someone else as better than himself. He encouraged me so incredibly much by doing something that was not common in his culture, because he wanted to spare his wife's hands. He demonstrated beautifully servant leadership, and authority. I greatly learned from them as a couple.

A Bad Example: "The Wrong Advice from an Elder"

In a totally different season in my life, I was thrown into a scenario that I was incredibly nervous about. Having been married for some time at this point, my wife and I were invited over to a family's house from our church (at that time).

When we arrived to fellowship with them we sat down in the living room. I sat down to relax in my comfy chair next to the father in the house. When my eyes looked up, I noticed a very pagan object standing in the opposite corner of the living room. My Spirit gasped, and I grieved with horrid grief about it. I knew in my heart this object needed to be dealt with. It was horrific, pagan, and I knew I should say something about it later. Furthermore, there were many things going on in their house, that could be potentially connected to this pagan object as an opening or doorway. The zeal of the Lord took a grasp of my heart, so I consulted an elder over me as what to do. When I went to this particular elder the advice he gave me was, "Don't worry about it, I wouldn't say anything about it." Those were his exact words, however he most likely based his decision off of a failed attempt at something I said earlier to this same family. After chewing on his thoughts for quite some time, my Spirit kept pressing. I knew that I should speak about that matter, directly to that brother and his family. So after some time I pressed forward and wrote my whole heart out on paper to this family about the pagan idol (with plenty of true research information), and sent it to the family. (However to be accountable I did inform the elder that I addressed the matter.) Not a day later he responded back with Amazing Gratitude, and got rid of the object immediately! He thanked me profusely for coming to him about it, and how tenderly I spoke to him. Since then he has even become closer to me than a brother, and his family is healing quite well, Praise the Lord! If I would have listened to the advice of the Elder in that situation, the brother would have still been in bondage with a Pagan Idol in his household. Though this doesn't paint the elder in the best light, sometimes we have to do things that are contrary to what we hear from Man. It is better to obey God, than Man.

Moving on to the next section, it is exceedingly important for us to acknowledge the types of authority that have been put into place in our lives. It is important to reveal the differences of authority that are active today in the church and sphere of life where we live. There is church authority and social authority, and with both we need to know the Lord's heart. However, inside of the church body there are differences between authority, opinions, commandments, and traditions.

In this next section I wish to illustrate the differences between these, and how they affect you. First and foremost, one of the most important things to realize is that God has placed rulers and authorities over us in the lands we live in. This can be classified as our "social authority" or "governing *authority*".

Scripture states the following:

Social Authority & Governing Authority

Let every person be subject to the governing authorities. For there is no authority except from God, and those that exist have been instituted by God. Therefore whoever resists the authorities resists what God has appointed, and those who resist will incur judgment. For rulers are not a terror to good conduct, but to bad. Would you have no fear of the one who is in authority? Then do what is good, and you will receive his approval, for he is God's servant for your good. But if you do wrong, be afraid, for he does not bear the sword in vain. For he is the servant of God, an avenger who carries out God's wrath on the wrongdoer. Therefore one must be in subjection, not only to avoid God's wrath but also for the sake of conscience. For because of this you also pay taxes, for the authorities are ministers of God, attending to this very thing. Pay to all what is owed to them: taxes to whom taxes are owed, revenue to whom revenue is owed, respect to whom respect is owed, honor to whom honor is owed.

Romans 13:1–7

Tell us, then, what you think. Is it lawful to pay taxes to Caesar, or not?" But Jesus, aware of their malice, said, "Why put me to the test, you hypocrites? Show me the coin for the tax." And they brought him a denarius.

And Jesus said to them, "Whose likeness and inscription is this?" They said, "Caesar's." Then he said to them,

"Therefore render to Caesar the things that are Caesar's, and to God the things that are God's.

Matthew 22:17-21

Keep your conduct among the Gentiles honorable, so that when they speak against you as evildoers, they may see your good deeds and glorify God on the day of visitation. Be subject for the Lord's sake to every human institution, whether it be to the emperor as supreme, or to governors as sent by him to punish those who do evil and to praise those who do good. For this is the will of God, that by doing good you should put to silence the ignorance of foolish people. Live as people who are free, not using your freedom as a cover-up for evil, but living as servants of God. Honor everyone. Love the brotherhood. Fear God. Honor the emperor.

1 Peter 2:12-17

Our social and governing authority is placed over us directly by God. They are not a mistake, for God does not make mistakes. No matter how good they are, or how wicked they are, God has allowed them to be in office.

We are commanded by scripture to honor them, and be obedient in all things. Meaning, we should pay our taxes, follow correctly the red lights, pay our bills, obey the police men, and maintain a walk of ethics and dignity so that the Gentiles, and non-believers will not reject God by our choices. The only time we are to disobey our Social Authorities is in the matter of compromise to the Scriptures. We must be willing to go to jail if they ask us to deny God, our faith, or Jesus. Compromise in these areas are not an option. We must obey God at all costs and not deny him due to Social pressure. But in all other situations of normal living, we are to follow every ordinance as placed upon us by the Governing Authority. Not some of the ordinances, ALL, even if they are burdensome and heavy.

Jesus himself told them, render to Caesar what is due him. We must be careful and heed scriptures correctly in this way especially. There are many "Christians" who do not like the leadership that is over them, so they oppose and remove the authority of that leadership. We have all been guilty of disrespecting, and dishonoring our Social Authority, and we must repent from this and change. I would agree that much of our current leadership is questionable, but that does not give us the right to pick and choose what laws to obey. The scripture is clear on this matter, and many people have started to isolate, and remove themselves from the due responsibility to their Authority. We honor God, while we honor our Authorities, even if we wear a heavy yoke.

Church Authority:

In this next section let's define some of the basic areas of Church Authority that you should be aware of. The basic groups are: Commandments of Scripture, Opinions of People, Traditions of Man. Most of what you will hear from the platform will fall into 1 of these 3 areas. And there is a great difference between them. Make no mistake, the Commands of Scripture are Full Authority, these are to be submitted to. However opinions of people, and traditions of man, are optional, and not law. I will try to reveal the difference between these briefly in the following section.

"Commandments of Scripture"

There are many commandments of Scripture but they are best summed up with a few important foundational verses.

"Teacher, which is the great commandment in the Law?"

And he said to him, "You shall love the Lord your God with all your heart and with all your soul and with all your mind. This is the great and first commandment. And a second is like it: You shall love your neighbor as yourself. On these two commandments depend all the Law and the Prophets."

Matthew 22:36–40

All Scripture is breathed out by God and profitable for teaching, for reproof, for correction, and for training in righteousness, that the man of God may be complete, equipped for every good work.

2 Timothy 3:16-17

There are several commandments in scriptures, it is important for us to know the heart about them. When any leader in a church setting advises you "Correctly" from scripture it is your responsibility to adhere and follow it correctly. This is not a difficult topic to understand. Obey God's word through God's appointed Authority in your life. These cannot be separated.

"Opinions & Extra-Biblical Traditions of Man"

Since you have been given a free will, you have the right to choose. The reality is God desires Authority to function correctly. If you are a good leader then you will clearly reveal to your sheep the heart of God. If you are a bad leader then you will veil God's heart, thus leaving the sheep blind and undernourished. We can never use our personal opinions as the Commandments of the Lord. Nor can we make our extra-Biblical traditions bring guilt upon those who do not follow them. Leadership take warning, your place of position is to unveil God's heart, not divert it. If you follow the countenance of Scripture you do well. If you mix your opinions and traditions into the word of God, you bring a tainted message. Here is what scripture says about *"Opinions and Traditions"* used wrongly.

Then Pharisees and scribes came to Jesus from Jerusalem and said, "Why do your disciples break the tradition of the elders? For they do not wash their hands when they eat." He answered them, "And why do you break the commandment of God for the sake of your tradition? For God commanded, 'Honor your father and your mother,' and, 'Whoever reviles father or mother must surely die.' But you say, 'If anyone tells his father or his mother, "What you would have gained from me is given to God," he need not honor his father.' So for the sake of your tradition you have made void the word of God.

Matthew 15:1-6

And the Lord said: "Because this people draw near with their mouth and honor me with their lips, while their hearts are far from me, and their fear of me is a commandment taught by men..."

Isaiah 29:13

Therefore, as you received Christ Jesus the Lord, so walk in him, rooted and built up in him and established in the faith, just as you were taught, abounding in thanksgiving. See to it that no one takes you captive by philosophy and empty deceit, according to human tradition, according to the elemental spirits of the world, and not according to Christ.

Colossians 2:6-8

As I have mentioned before you cannot command people to fear God out of tradition. God has to teach this through the Spirit. The Pharisees were full of ordinances, traditions, and laws that tried to bring about Righteousness to no avail. These became taxing, and overbearing on the people. However not all ordinances and traditions are bad. There are many times where they serve as protection to us walking in the body. This is why we must use discernment when we do use ordinances and traditions in their rightful places. Knowing God's view on Authority, and how to walk in it is your protection as a believer. If you choose to walk outside of God's authority, you put yourself in danger. We cannot be wilderness prophets, we must be connected to the body, with Christ as our Head. Your safety is submission under authority as often as possible.

There are many Christians today that get fearful when they hear the words, *"Submit"* and *"Authority"*. Rightfully so! Many have been hurt in church splits, and bad relationships from the very authority that they were supposed to submit to. So to them, submission to authority is pain and death. But let me bid you this: submission to authority provides every believer both protection and covering.

There are many today in the body of Christ that have removed themselves out of any position to walk under authority for fear of being hurt. As I have mentioned these are independent wilderness walkers. They claim the Holy Spirit as their authority and say, "Man only messes things up." I will not deny that man is fallible, but that gives no right to deny that God has put man in authority. His reason is for protection.

> *Obey your leaders and submit to them, for they are keeping watch over your souls, as those who will have to give an account. Let them do this with joy and not with groaning, for that would be of no advantage to you.*
>
> *Hebrews 13:17*

> *Likewise, you who are younger, be subject to the elders. Clothe yourselves, all of you, with humility toward one another, for "God opposes the proud but gives grace to the humble.*
>
> *1 Peter 5:5*

We all have experienced plenty of examples of both good and bad authority. That being the case, there are many churches to choose from in which we need to be wise in hearing the Spirit's direction. Therefore, it is vitally important for you to know from God, why you walk where you do. If God has you in a place like he did with Samuel, then you cannot leave that place. God sometimes places us in situations with faulty leadership. Not as a word from the Lord, but my own opinion is this: "If you can submit to and walk under authority that is not 100% correct how much more can, and will you, walk under and submit to God's authority which is

100% absolute." Samuel was strengthened while serving under imperfect leadership, and he became strong in the Lord. We can expect the same. If you are faithful to submission, you will be faithful to being a leader. Leaders are formed and tried in different seasons under varying leadership's where their level of submission and commitment is tested. True authority comes from an individual that has submerged himself in submission.

However if God has not told you emphatically to stay under that leader, that is bad, then you have every right to look and find another quality place of authority to be under. It is very important to know the leadership when you are picking out a place to join and walk with. Let me adamantly encourage you to pay attention to the character traits of your leaders. A true leader will never use flattery, deception, baiting, vanity, or false hope to control your life. Many leaders use these things, to lord over you and control your life wrongly.

Be aware and watchful, God's true leaders will be walking with you humbly at the foot of the Cross of Jesus. Authority is for your edification and not your destruction (2 Corinthians 10:8). Therefore if the authority is using these worldly means to snag you, or use you, it will be your destruction. Don't let vain words puff your head, EVER!

> My sheep know my voice, and I know them and they follow me.
>
> John 10:27

Words of flattery, and vanity are not the voice of the Lord. Wrong leaders use these words to manipulate and draw followers to themselves. If you give yourself to wrong authorities you start to walk down a very dangerous road. We are to follow the voice of Jesus only, and when you hear that in a leader you will stay there.

In Conclusion, God has established Authority and Order to be followed by us. The perfect order of the Trinity is demonstrated through the perfect "Intended" order of the Church. God is functioning correctly, though at times the church is not. Remember whether you walk in a church body currently or not, Jesus is the Head, and he has all authority. My prayer is that you use discernment, and the voice of the Spirit to guide you into the proper place to serve the Lord in. Taking into consideration the things that have been mentioned in this chapter, you will do well to find pure, humble, authority. But if God has not released you to go somewhere else, walk in obedience where you are as best as you can. It is in the heart that God wants to grow and perfect obedience. In this place God will show you how to walk under authority and in authority. There is no other place to walk. My prayer is that you succeed in this very large classroom of growth.

> *There is a difference between being a radical loose cannon and a mighty tempered stallion in the control of the Holy Spirit. Which one are you?*

Section 2

Victory in the Anointed Tongue

CHAPTER SIX

The Language Of Prophecy

Now that you have seen the foundations of prophecy let's transition into the function of the tongue in prophecy. For this entire next section I am going to discuss matters that relate to the tongue. The tongue of a prophet needs to function correctly and in its right place, if not then much damage is done. My goal in this next chapter is to discuss the terminology in which prophecy most frequently functions.

Now that we know the heart of prophecy points to Jesus, in this chapter I would like to discuss the tone and language of prophecy. This topic is important for all functions in the body of Christ, not just the prophetic person. For this applies also to pastors, evangelists, teachers, and apostles. Regardless of our position or function in Christ, each of us needs to walk in a correct language when speaking to fellow believers about their lives. This chapter can be summed up in seven major words used in the New Testament. I will define them one by one, and briefly discuss them before we move on to the final thoughts for this chapter. The seven major words are: "Exhortation, Edification, Comfort, Admonish, Rebuke, Warn, Reprove". Though seven have been picked to define and discuss, three of them are indeed the foundation, while the other 4 are directly connected to this foundation and are also found in scripture.

> *But he that prophesieth speaketh unto men to edification, and exhortation, and comfort.*
>
> 1 Corinthians 14:3 (KJV)

> *I charge you in the presence of God and of Christ Jesus, who is to judge the living and the dead, and by his appearing and his kingdom: preach the word; be ready in season and out of season; reprove, rebuke, and exhort, with complete patience and teaching.*
>
> 2 Timothy 4:1-2

Word # 1–"Exhort, Exhortation"

Greek Definitions

G3870–PARAKALEO - To call to one's side, to address, to beg, to plead to, to instruct, to teach, console.

G3867–PARAINEO - To exhort, to admonish, from to praise.

G3874–PARAKLESIS - A calling near (especially for help), supplication, and refreshment, stirring address, powerful discourse.

G3056–LOGOS - A word uttered by a living voice, speaking forth, something said aloud, to break silence.

Vine's Dictionary - Primarily to call a person, to call on entreat, to urge someone to pursue some source of conduct, looking to the future, as opposed with comfort which has to do in retrospective trial experience.

With PARAINEO to speak of near, to advise, warn. With POTREPO, to turn forward, propel, to urge forward. With PARAKLESIS, a calling to one's side, and so to one's aid, encouragement, advocate, comforter.

Webster's & 1828 (Version)- To urge, advise, or caution earnestly, admonish urgently, to give urgent advise, recommendations, warnings. To incite by words or advice; to animate or urge by arguments to a good deed or to any laudable conduct or course of action. The primary sense seems to be to excite or to give strength, spirit or courage.

As a note the Greek word for Exhortation and Holy Spirit are very similar. This is beautiful to notice because the Holy Spirit wishes to come along side of us with His exhortation, if we are willing to listen.

Word # 2–"Comfort"

Greek Definitions

G3889–PARAMUTHIA – Any address, whether made for the purpose of persuading, or of arousing, stimulating, or calming and consoling.

Vine's Dictionary–Primarily a speaking closely to anyone, hence denotes consolation, comfort, with a greater degree of tenderness than that of exhortation. With PAREGORIA, primarily an addressing, address, hence denotes a soothing, solace. A verbal form of the word signifies medicines, which allay irritation.

Webster's – 1. To strengthen; to invigorate; to cheer or enliven. 2. To strengthen the mind when depressed or enfeebled; to console; to give new vigor to the spirits; to cheer, or relieve from depression, or trouble. 3. In law, to relieve, assist or encourage, as the accessory to a crime after the fact.

As a note let's especially take notice of the 3rd definition in Webster's. This is very similar to the word admonish which we will see in a bit. For the majority it can be said that the idea of "Comforting" someone is truly a medicine for the soul.

Word # 3 – "Edify, Edification"

Greek Definitions

G3618–OIKODOMEO - To build a house, to restore, to found, to establish, to promote Christian growth.

G3619–OIKODOME - The act of building a house, the act of establishing a house, edification.

G3622–OIKONOMIA - Management of a household, administration, office of overseer.

Vine's – This word is only used figuratively in the New Testament. It seems to be compared to spiritual growth. In one instance the Apostle renders it towards a brother with a weak conscience. Essentially anything in a figurative or literal sense.

Theological Dictionary – Literally means to build, though in some instances it could refer to planting. Paul may destroy when necessary, but his true work was to build up. This is also seen as a community task. Love, however always serves to edify. It is also suggested that by the use of speaking in tongues that is Self Edification, and Prophecy serves to edify the community.

Webster's – To instruct or benefit, especially morally or spiritually, to uplift, to enlighten.

Word # 4–"Admonish, Admonishment"

Greek Definitions

G3559–NOUTHESIA - Calling attention to, mild rebuke warning.

G3560–NOUTHETEO - To put in mind, reprove gently, caution.

Hebrew Definitions

H2094–ZAHAR - Warn, teach, shine, send out light (fig.).

H5749–UD   -   To return, to bear witness, enjoin solemnly.

Vine's – The difference between admonish and teach, seems to be that whereas the former has mainly in view the things that are wrong and call for warning, the latter has to do chiefly with the impartation of positive truth. To give advise often in a business sense. Basically it can be said, "The training by word".

Theological Dictionary - To impart understanding, to set right, to lay on the heart. The stress is no merely on the intellect but the will and disposition. It describes a basic means of education. The idea is not that of punishment but of moral appeal that leads to amendment. To reprimand, to correct. Philo represents divine warnings as distinct from divine punishments. The verb denotes a pastoral function.

Webster - To caution, advise or counsel against something, to reprove or scold, especially in a mild and good willed manner, to urge or remind of obligation.

A side note – Admonish is used when a wrong action has been taken, to re-teach correctly.

Word # 5–"Rebuke, Rebuking"

Greek Definitions

G2008–EPITIMAO   -   To show honor, to raise prize, to award in the sense of a merited penalty, to charge sharply.

G1651–ELEGCHO   -   To convict, to find fault, to chasten to punish, to tell a fault.

Hebrew Definitions

H1605–GAAR   -   To rebuke, to corrupt, to reprove.

H3198–YAWKAKH   -   To correct, to chasten, to be reproved.

Vine's - To put honor upon , then to adjudge, hence signifies rebuke. Whereas in the case of the word EPIPLESSO it states, "to strike at, or smite".

Theological Dictionary – At first usage suggests, to punish, to condemn, or convict, even to examine. It often denotes God's disciplining by teaching, admonition. It also states "to show people their sins and summon them to repentance, either privately or congregationally.

In the second usage of the word it is suggested that EPITIMAO is generally applied to God's rebuke, and in a limited way to a human rebuke, but, one believer may rebuke another if it is done in a spirit of forgiveness. Though this suggests human rebuke with great reserve. Though there is a sense of congregational correction and punishment/censure used with the form EPITIMIA.

Strong's- On PLESSO, it is the idea of flattening out, to pound to inflict with calamity, to smite.

Webster's–To express sharp, stern disapproval of, reprove, reprimand, a sharp reproof.

A side note- Out of all 7 words used the word Rebuke is by far the sharpest Chastisement. Even though it is severe, it can be accomplished with the correct goal in mind: that of Redemption.

Word # 6–"Warn"

Greek Definitions

G3559–NOUTHESIA - Calling attention to, mild rebuke warning.

G3560–NOUTHETEO - To put in mind, reprove gently, caution.

Hebrew Definitions

H2094–ZAHAR   - To admonish, warn, teach, shine, send out light, be light, be shining.

Vine's – To put in mind, warn, primarily to show secretly, generally to teach or make know.

Webster's –"To give notice of approaching or probable danger or evil, that it may be avoided; to caution against any thing that may prove injurious. To caution against evil practices. To admonish of any duty."

A side note- Warn is very similar to the word Admonish. There is not much difference. It is a variance between writers and knowledge of the Greek Language.

Word # 7–"Reprove"

Greek Definitions

G1651–ELEGCHO – To convict, to find fault, to chasten to punish, to tell a fault.

Hebrew Definitions

H3198–YAWKAKH - To correct, to chasten, to be reprove.

Webster's – 1. To blame; to censure. 2. To charge with a fault to the face; to chide; to reprehend. 3. To blame for; with of; as, to reprove one of laziness. 4. To convince of a fault, or to make it manifest. 5. To refute; to disprove. 6. To excite a sense of guilt. The heart or conscience reproves us. 7. To manifest silent disapprobation or blame.

A side note–This word is also a synonym for rebuke. Therefore this places the idea of a reprove in the same intensity as rebuke. Regardless if done in correct manner, he who receives a good rebuke will grow from it.

After looking in depth to what these words mean, we see very clearly a variance of tones and situational timing. While some words like comfort are used very tenderly, there are others on the other extreme like rebuke that are used sharply. The ones in the middle like admonish, and warn can be compared to retaking an exam you failed, in an educational sense. "Johnny you messed up on this math equation let's do it better next time." Regardless these are all words to be used in maintenance and protection of the Christian believer. They are used as protection, with the intention of correction, either before a failure, during a failure, or after. As an emphatic "Warning" from me to you, use the right tone, in the right season. For example, if you are about to rebuke someone for a sin that he has committed, you better have the heart of the Spirit before hand, because there may be a chance that the Spirit intended that brother to be "Comforted" instead of "Rebuked". The Holy Spirit is the one who discerns where the heart is, and we must follow his leading and prompting.

However the goal is to actively speak words of Truth to all clearly and correctly. The Bible encourages us in this way. Speaking prophetically is not a complacent, lethargic responsibility, it is active one.

> *... But exhort one another daily, while it is called Today;*
> *lest any of you be hardened through the deceitfulness of sin.*
> *Hebrews 3:13 (KJV)*

If we are daily on guard, both in our personal communion and corporate fellowship, sin will not be able to creep in to our lives. However our society has twisted in so many ways that "Active Exhortation" is considered being "Over Spiritual". However this topic will be discussed in a later chapter. Regardless we must be concerned daily for each other in the light of truth and exhortation. If we do not, then consciences will sear, standards will fail, and no one will listen anymore to truth. To give a beautiful natural example of daily exhortation and maintenance let's take a look at the DNA strand.

I have come into knowledge about a particular cell that functions only on the DNA strand. Its only purpose is to go up and down all day long on the DNA strand. Sounds like a boring job, but it is a vital job for your body to function correctly. This cell moves up and down on the DNA strand looking for holes, gaps, flaws, and incomplete sections of the DNA. Once at that particular section it then proceeds to fix it. What an absolutely gorgeous picture of Exhorting one another Daily. True Science reveals God heart always. This cell is very similar to the function of a prophet. The prophet has been given the job to see what's wrong and bring appropriate light and correction to the affected area. The prophet has been given eyesight to see a crack and fill it correctly, so that the building will stand and be strong.

God wants his church body to be strong and edified. Edification is the figure of speech that is often used in the Bible for building. Sometimes we come to a situation and the wall is broken down, and in need of repair. This is where mortar is needed. Just like in the DNA strand, the cell is assigned to edify it. This repairing cell uses good cells or "Mortar" to build up the DNA strand. God intends for the same in the body of Christ. We must edify the breaches correctly by filling in the gaps. But there are places in the Bible that reveal what happens when they are not filled correctly.

O Israel, thy prophets are like the foxes in the deserts. Ye have not gone up into the gaps, neither made up the hedge for the house of Israel to stand in the battle in the day of the LORD. They have seen vanity and lying divination, saying, The LORD saith: and the LORD hath not sent them: and they have made others to hope that they would confirm the word. Have ye not seen a vain vision, and have ye not spoken a lying divination, whereas ye say, The LORD saith it; albeit I have not spoken?

Therefore thus saith the Lord GOD; Because ye have spoken vanity, and seen lies, therefore, behold, I am against you, saith the Lord GOD. And mine hand shall be upon the prophets that see vanity,and that divine lies: they shall not be in the assembly of my people, neither shall they be written in the writing of the house of Israel, neither shall they enter into the land of Israel; and ye shall know that I am the Lord GOD. Because, even because they have seduced my people, saying,Peace; and there was no peace; and one built up a wall, and, lo, others daubed it with untempered morter: Say unto them which daub it with untempered morter, that it shall fall: there shall be an overflowing shower; and ye, O great hailstones, shall fall; and a stormy wind shall rend it. Lo, when the wall is fallen, shall it not be said unto you, Where is the daubing wherewith ye have daubed it? Therefore thus saith the Lord GOD; I will even rend it with a stormy wind in my fury; and there shall be an overflowing shower in mine anger, and great hailstones in my fury to consume it. So will I break down the wall that ye have daubed with untempered morter, and bring it down to the ground, so that the foundation thereof shall be discovered, and it shall fall, and ye shall be consumed in the midst thereof: and ye shall know that I am the LORD. Thus will I accomplish my wrath upon the wall, and upon them that have daubed it with untempered morter, and will say unto you, The wall is no more, neither they that daubed it; To wit, the prophets of Israel which prophesy concerning Jerusalem, and which see visions of peace for her, and there is no peace, saith the Lord GOD.

Ezekiel 13:4-16 (KJV)

So in this story the false prophets used fake words, lies, and self imposed building projects, that left the real city in danger, and in ruin. As it has been spoken of in a previous chapter, words of flattery, are inexcusable. If you use mortar that is filled with deceit or flattery your cracks will only grow bigger. As these above prophets spoke peace and safety, they caused a city to fall and be destroyed. Their untempered mortar was untrue, invalid, and faulty. God was not pleased with these men who presumed to help the people. "Faithful are the wounds of a friend; but the kisses of an enemy are deceitful," (Proverbs 27:6 KJV).

In a world of rebellion, sarcasm, and deceitfulness it is hard to come by pure truth. But truth is what we need most. I have heard someone say, "Your best friend is the one who tells you the most truth". That is the great need in our day. A true friend will bring correction out of love when you are in the wrong, or in danger.

His words may feel like they wound you, but faithful are those wounds in the end to heal and build you up, unlike the enemy who will kiss you with deceitfulness. He yells "Peace, Peace" when there is no peace. His kisses only lead to death, and destruction. If your building is in need of major repair, don't walk around as if nothing is wrong. You will be acting like there is Peace, when there is none. Be thankful for those friends who do speak into your life truthfully. The problem is many people despise truth, and don't want to listen to it. This is where our society has come. History is repeating itself again.

The heart behind prophecy is to speak the truth for the purpose of rebuilding. Just because someone is speaking truth to you does not mean they hate you. Often the truest form of love is speaking the truth. The problem is people accuse prophetic people of judging. They say, "Don't judge me, who are you to say something like that to me. Only God can judge me." This will be discussed also in a later chapter. Though for now the current topic is about a problem in our society of people who don't want to listen to truth. The Bible is very clear about right judgment and wrong judgment. But for this chapter it is important to bring out the fact that there is a drastic difference between Condemnation & Reproof. These lines have been blurred and are being used to prevent the voice of prophecy in many places. But we must not be silent.

Judgment as in Webster's..."The determination of the mind, formed from comparing the relations of ideas, or the comparison of facts and arguments. In the formation of our judgments, we should be careful to weigh and compare all the facts connected with the subject. In law, the sentence of doom pronounced in any cause, civil or criminal, by the judge or court by which it is tried. Judgment may be rendered on demurrer, on a verdict, on a confession or default, or on a non-suit. Judgment, though pronounced by the judge or court, is properly the determination or sentence of the law. A pardon may be pleaded in arrest of judgment. The right or power of passing sentence. determination; decision."

Because the lines have been blurred so bad in our society it is important for us to see judgment in the light of what Scripture says about it. Consider the following verses.

> *Judge not, that you be not judged. For with the judgment you pronounce you will be judged, and with the measure you use it will be measured to you. Why do you see the speck that is in your brother's eye, but do not notice the log that is in your own eye? Or how can you say to your brother, 'Let me take the speck out of your eye,' when there is the log in your own eye? You hypocrite, first take the log out of your own eye, and then you will see clearly to take the speck out of your brother's eye.*

> *Matthew 7:1-5*

All of us could spend hours trying to find the full exegetical meaning of this scripture, but it is not my point or purpose at this time. There are several other scriptures that speak about proper judgment as well, as righteous judgment. Those too, I will not speak about here. In context this passage is talking about Hypocrisy. My point in this passage is verse 5. "First take the log out of your own eye, and then you will see clearly to take the speck out of your brother's eye." As it has been mentioned in a previous chapter, you can speak to a brother about a particular issue, but if you are struggling with that same sin, it is not the time for you to address it with anyone else.

If you are free from it, then speak with all boldness and gentleness. Many stop at the first part of this verse and build their case from it. However the verse does finish with revealing the proper outcome of the matter. In the beginning one brother saw a speck in another brother's eye. He wanted to remove the speck out of his brother's eye, but could not do so because of the log in his own. Only after his eye was healed could he properly heal the other brother's eye. The goal was that both eyes were to be clean and clear.

From Webster's definition, we see the reality of judgment explained before our eyes. It is basically summed up in two ways: 1. "Judgment leading towards condemnation or a sentence, and the other is 2. Judgment leading one to a final discernment on a matter." These are the two lines that have blurred in our society. Let me simply explain how these two differ. If you go to a brother who is in sin, and you tell him, "May your house burn down, for your iniquity!" This is a judgment leading to condemnation. But if you go to that brother and say, "You are in sin, and I fear the consequences if you do not repent and turn from your sin!" This is a discerning judgment, that is not a condemnation.

The goal is not to destroy the brother or his property, the goal is to redeem the brother! This latter is a proper Judgment that leads to life. It was an "Assessment" of the situation, with the intention of Redemption. This second definition is really how it is done correctly in light of scriptures, and in good conscience. It is totally ok to "Assess" a matter and weigh the truth in your mind about a sin issue.

The Holy Spirit will guide you in your "Assessment" and give you wisdom on how to address it. That is "IF" you are to address it. The problem is most people know judgment as the first definition, and this proves to be problematic for a prophetic individual.

If we would just remember the scripture that says...

> *...And do not get drunk with wine, for that is debauchery, but be filled with the Spirit, addressing one another in psalms and hymns and spiritual songs,*

> *singing and making melody to the Lord with your heart,*
> *giving thanks always and for everything to God the*
> *Father in the name of our Lord Jesus Christ, submitting*
> *to one another in the fear of God.*
>
> *Ephesians 5:18-21*

Speaking to others would be easier if one would submit to listen. The problem is people have put themselves in varying places of "service in ministry" where they cannot be touched, nor have to submit one to another. Jesus walked as a servant among the disciples and his followers. Jesus, the best example of leadership ever known to man, demonstrated both submission and humility. He taught the disciples that to lead, they must serve. He rebuked and exhorted them when they wanted to climb a Spiritual Ladder. The whole goal of everything Jesus taught to the disciples was to be humble, and love others. Now thousands of years later we have untouchable leadership, and untouchable sheep. This is not the reality of the true New Testament Church. If a baby Christian walks up to one of us to exhort or reprove us about a matter, we have to be willing to listen and humble ourselves in submission of their word. If their word is not in accord with the Spirit, Scripture, or the heart of God, then we can dismiss it tenderly. But if it is in accord with the Spirit, Scripture, and the heart of God we must receive and act upon it. It does not matter the age, status, or maturity of the individual bringing the word, because if it is from God, his word will not return void. The same goes for any leader in any church, anywhere, you MUST be able to hear from any sheep at anytime. If you cannot, you have exalted yourself above the normal path we walk on as Christians. Everything is level at the foot of the cross.

As a reminder there are warnings in scripture to all of us on how to exhort those older than us, and to these warnings we should take heed.

In conclusion for this chapter it can be said simply, that you must know the right language to speak in, at the right time, with the right outcome.

The language of prophecy will only be profitable to you if you are walking submerged in the Word, and in the anointing of the Spirit. The goal of the world is to keep you silent, the goal of the Spirit is to have you speak with an Anointed Tongue. Though there will be resistance to any form of truth, you must press forward without regret. Whether the matter is about sin, a gap in the wall, or a potential pot hole ahead, the voice of truth must go forth because prophecy is for the church body of Christ.

He who speaks in a tongue edifies himself, but he who prophesies edifies the church.

> *...therefore tongues are for a sign, not to those who believe but to unbelievers; but prophesying is not for unbelievers but for those who believe.*
>
> *1 Corinthians 14: 4, 22 (NKJV)*

As clear as I personally can say to you, speak correctly! When someone needs to be rebuked, do it sharply and in love and redemption. If someone needs to have a word of comfort, love them graciously with utter tenderness. Either way whether you use a strong word, or a gentle word, we are to be a doctor with a scalpel in the midst of broken people, not a warrior with a sword in the midst of his enemies. God wants to fix his people, not slay them. Speak the truth in love at all times.

> *Silence about sin, is one of the greatest*
> *dangers to any Christian walk.*

CHAPTER SEVEN

Words–They All Count!

The bridle is off and the harness is gone on the human tongue. Our society has devalued our speech to such a desolate place, that real words have lost their value. Many other words have turned to vulgar expression. The human tongue in our current society flaps like a flag in gale force winds with no sight of daylight. But, for the prophetic tongue this cannot be. In God's Kingdom, every word counts!

If God has called you to minister in the body of Christ Jesus, he has also called your tongue to be properly bridled, both in and out of the pulpit. You are held to a higher standard as you are an oracle of God. You are now required to take active inventory of the words you speak. Even for those who are not called into active ministry, these same exhortations of scripture apply to our everyday life. Words are no longer a dime a dozen for our society, they are a penny for a million. Human words are so very cheap, but for God's children and messengers they simply must carry the weight and value of a higher road and calling.

God spoke a simple word and all life and mankind came into being. God's powerful words are the foundations of all we know and will know. His almighty words are not to be taken lightly. Therefore since His words will not return void, his desire is that his servants words will not be void either. This is why we must examine the types of words we use. If you look at scriptures correctly the words that we speak can be categorized into 3 main sections. Though not all, these are the three main topics I would like to discuss in this chapter. They are 1. Perverse Words 2. Wasteful Words 3. Useful Words. All speech in which we partake, will fall into one of these three categories. There is honestly no gray area on this matter.

Category # 1–Perverse or Ill-Intentioned Words

In this category we can find several words that meet these criteria. It is easy to know by scripture and by conscience what words belong in this category. These words include; Corrupt, Vulgar, Evil, Cursing, Perverted, Sensual, Slanderous, Rebellious, Coarse, Racial, and the list can go on and on. These words are all words that clearly have the essence of an evil heart, intent to defame, disgrace, and destroy. Most of these words we can easily detect in the world, but lately even in the church.

Here are a few places in scripture that speak about the usage of these words.

> *Therefore be imitators of God, as beloved children. And walk in love, as Christ loved us and gave himself up for us, a fragrant offering and sacrifice to God. But sexual immorality and all impurity or covetousness must not even be named among you, as is proper among saints. Let there be no filthiness nor foolish talk nor crude joking, which are out of place, but instead let there be thanksgiving.*
>
> *Ephesians 5:1-4*

Let no corrupt communication proceed out of your mouth, but that which is good to the use of edifying, that it may minister grace unto the hearers.

Ephesians 4:29 (KJV)

O Timothy, keep that which is committed to thy trust, avoiding profane and vain babblings, and oppositions of science falsely so called: Which some professing have erred concerning the faith. Grace be with thee. Amen.

1 Timothy 6:20-21(KJV)

Do not speak evil against one another, brothers. The one who speaks against a brother or judges his brother, speaks evil against the law and judges the law. But if you judge the law, you are not a doer of the law but a judge.

James 4:11

Keep your tongue from evil and your lips from speaking deceit.

Psalms 34:13

For "Whoever desires to love life and see good days, let him keep his tongue from evil and his lips from speaking deceit; let him turn away from evil and do good; let him seek peace and pursue it. For the eyes of the Lord are on the righteous, and his ears are open to their prayer. But the face of the Lord is against those who do evil.

1 Peter 3:10-12

For it is shameful even to speak of the things that they
do in secret,

Ephesians 5:12

So as a recap for this first category, any words or conversation that have evil intentions, negative outcome, vulgarity, perversions, or any of the like, are not supposed to be coming out of the Christian mouth whatsoever. Period.

Category # 2–Wasteful & Worthless Words

Surprisingly, this category is the one that will shock people the most. Many people will say they don't have a vulgar mouth, but that is not the only problem of the human tongue.

In this category, let's talk about the speech in scripture that is referred to as Worthless & Wasteful. The words that fit into this category are words like, idle words, desolate words, useless, unfruitful, vain, and foolish. Here are several references that talk about these types of words. Some verses may repeat from the above section.

O men, how long shall my honor be turned into shame?
How long will you love vain words and seek after lies? Selah.

Psalms 4:2

Let there more work be laid upon the men, that they
may labour therein; and let them not regard vain words.

Exodus 5:9 (KJV)

Thou shalt not take the name of the LORD thy God in
vain; for the LORD will not hold him guiltless that taketh
his name in vain.

Exodus 20:7 (KJV)

Neither filthiness, nor foolish talking, nor jesting, which are not convenient: but rather giving of thanks.

Ephesians 5:4 (KJV)

Certain persons, by swerving from these, have wandered away into vain discussion, desiring to be teachers of the law, without understanding either what they are saying or the things about which they make confident assertions.

1 Timothy 1:6-7

...But avoid foolish questions, and genealogies, and contentions, and strivings about the law; for they are unprofitable and vain.

Titus 3:9 (KJV)

...But I say unto you, That every idle word that men shall speak, they shall give account thereof in the day of judgment. For by thy words thou shalt be justified, and by thy words thou shalt be condemned.

Matthew 12:36 (KJV)

To further bring light to this section it is important to add the definitions for vain and idle, so that we can see the heart more clearly in these passages.

Vain as defined in Webster's—"Empty; worthless; having no substance, value or importance, Fruitless; ineffectual. Empty; unsatisfying, Not effectual; having no efficacy. Also conceited."

Idle as defined in Webster's–"Remaining unused; unemployed; applied to things; as, my sword or spear is idle. Useless; vain; ineffectual; as idle rage. Unfruitful; barren; not productive of good."

This section is of utter importance for us to examine! Vulgar & perverse words are clearly visible and wrong, but the Lord also emphatically desires for each of our words to count in speech. Many conversations that we have today are worthless. If you sit and replay the things talked about throughout the day, you will find most words are of no value. When I say value, I mean for the Kingdom of God, or the edification of the Body. There are so many foolish and coarse jokes, that are not life giving. Worthless words with no value, are an offense to God, for his intent was to bring life and not death through words. We need to take these scriptures to heart and know that God wants all of our speech to mean something of eternal value or significance. This is why Jesus clearly stated that we will give an account for every idle word we speak!

There is also another highly important aspect to this matter that is important to discuss briefly. That is taking the Lord's name in vain. Vain and vulgar words are both despised by the Lord. So whether you are using the Lord's name as a swear word, or using the Lord's name with no value, both are considered wrong in the eyes of the Lord. If you look closely at these definitions, and the accounts of scripture it shows that not all Vain words are vulgar. Many vain words are worthless or empty. Really the heart behind the word vain, is to devalue, or take away importance and worth. What a huge population of Christians we have today who use the Lord's name in vain all day long, and don't even realize it. If someone says "G-D" it is clearly vulgar. But there are plenty of phrases and uses of the Lord's name that are vain in a worthless sense. Many of which include saying, "Oh My God, Oh Lord, Lordy Lordy, Oh God, and even the name of Jesus without actually talking to him. You all know what I am talking about here. These are wrong in God's eyes!

We have lost all touch with the reality of who God is. His name is powerful and beautiful, and we cannot say it without "Real Value"!

For example the scribes of old when writing and copying scriptures had to wash themselves each time before they even wrote the name of God. Now I am not trying to be legalistic about this, but it is important to bring into remembrance the honor and reverence that they had for the name of the Lord. We have lost this in our society, and it needs to be regained. Because scripture says at the name of Jesus every knee will bow. We must walk very carefully when we speak of God. His name is to be exalted and used with worth always!

Category #3–Useful & Life Giving Words

This is the safest place a Christian can use his/her mouth for the glory of the Lord, words that are useful, and full of redeeming Life! You cannot go wrong when you choose to speak with words of love, and edification. Here are a few reminders from scripture about this category.

Speaking to yourselves in psalms and hymns and spiritual songs, singing and making melody in your heart to the Lord; Giving thanks always for all things unto God and the Father in the name of our Lord Jesus Christ.

Ephesians 5:19-20 (KJV)

Let the word of Christ dwell in you richly in all wisdom; teaching and admonishing one another in psalms and hymns and spiritual songs, singing with grace in your hearts to the Lord. And whatsoever ye do in word or deed, do all in the name of the Lord Jesus, giving thanks to God and the Father by him.

Colossians 3:16-17 (KJV)

Therefore encourage one another and build one another up, just as you are doing. We ask you, brothers, to respect those who labor among you and are over you in the Lord and admonish you, and to esteem them very highly in love because of their work. Be at peace among yourselves. And we urge you, brothers, admonish the idle, encourage the fainthearted, help the weak, be patient with them all. See that no one repays anyone evil for evil, but always seek to do good to one another and to everyone.

1 Thessalonians 5:11-15

A word fitly spoken is like apples of gold in a setting of silver
Proverbs 25:11

There are plenty of other numerous verses in scripture that talk about speaking usefully and redemptive. Of course I cannot mention them all, but it is easy to see from scripture that our words are to have life in them. The reality is the tongue is very dangerous if not controlled by the Spirit. We will look at further details in another chapter about Blessing & Cursing with the tongue. However in this chapter the focal point is the everyday conversations of the tongue. Our daily choices of conversation reveal what is in our heart.

The tongue is the forgotten 5th chamber of the heart, and it works hand in glove with the heart. It functions like a teapot, whistling away as to what is cooking on the inside. The mouth and tongue are the signals of the soul's condition. It is true therefore that what proceeds out of the mouth proceeds from the heart.

The problem is that, "The Spiritual Immune System" of many Christians is not working. Their consciences have been seared like with a hot iron, and many don't even recognize the filth that is coming from their mouth. Sadly, many may not care either about this insensitivity.

The tongue not only reveals the language and tone of the heart, but it also reveals the agenda of the heart. If you are obsessed with sports, then that is all you will talk about. If you are obsessed with media and movies, then that will be your topic of conversation. However if the love of God fills your heart up full, then your mouth will be speaking about the wonders of God, and the hope of eternity with Jesus. The tongue exposes the intentions and treasures of the soul.

Who can stand if we are judged only by our tongue? No one!! Praise God for His longsuffering mercy for us. God works on us daily to rid us of a nasty, out of control tongue. As the Christian grows in Spirit led life the tongue will change from a death wielding, despicable, tramp of an animal, to a life giving, fruit filled, river of Heaven! You may have been a wretch of a person before you knew the Lord. You may have cussed like a sailor in the presence of your own mother, but when you meet God, your mouth will truly change! If you are walking in the life of Jesus Christ your mouth will change and clean up quicker than you think. The best cure for a potty mouth is to be washed with the word of Jesus Christ. A deluge of scripture with the real anointing of the Holy Spirit will bring about this change. No mouth is untamable for the Holy Spirit! Give the Holy Spirit the reigns of your mouth and you will grow towards pure, clean speech!

In conclusion for this chapter it is best to conclude by stating: every word that we speak needs to have value for God's kingdom. If you still have coarse jokes, and perverse language then you are greatly in need of the washing of the word. This manner of speaking is not fitting at all for those who call themselves Christians and Children of God. We are to be like minded, and speak words of life like Jesus.

If you cannot say your story, your joke, or any thought, in heaven in the presence of God, then neither should you say it here on earth. If you have gained great maturity in this area, then examine your words in other non-relevant social matters. Every day we live we need to pro-actively build and edify the Body with our words. The lifestyle of a Christian is not one of lethargy or complacency. This is why frivolous conversation of non-important thoughts are to also be monitored in light of the Spirit.

We live in a very dark society, and our word usage has dropped off the deep end. But this does not mean that you and I cannot return back again to quality speech, and quality edification. True it may be, we all may be alone in this attempt, but this is the heart of God. It is not impossible for victory over the tongue, and we must fight to get that victory! Being called prophetically, our language must know the victory of the tongue if we are to speak correctly.

Having therefore these promises, dearly beloved, let us cleanse ourselves from all filthiness of the flesh and spirit, perfecting holiness in the fear of God.

2 Corinthians 7:1 (KJV)

O generation of vipers, how can ye, being evil, speak good things? For out of the abundance of the heart the mouth speaketh. A good man out of the good treasure of the heart bringeth forth good things: and an evil man out of the evil treasure bringeth forth evil things. But I say unto you, That every idle word that men shall speak, they shall give account thereof in the day of judgment. For by thy words thou shalt be justified, and by thy words thou shalt be condemned.

Matthew 12:34–37 (KJV)

"God is not a man, that he should lie!"

Are we listening? Then let us take heed of his words of warning.

CHAPTER EIGHT

Ham Bone Soup

As we have seen in the first two chapters of this section, the tongue must be used correctly, and words must be spoken carefully. The tongue must carry an anointing from the Lord both as a leader, and as a follower. In this chapter the focus will be about our conversations with fellow believers in our daily walk. I will be using several illustrations and word pictures at the beginning of this chapter to paint and bring out better the truth and explanation of what is happening in the body of Christ. So let's begin with the illustration of "Southern" Ham Bone Soup.

If any of you have ever lived or visited the south for a long period of time, chances are you have had Ham Bone Soup. The southern folks have a great way of cooking and making broth for soup stocks. It's actually easy as pie to make. All you need is one good slab of Ham Bone. Usually this bone is the left over bone after a good holiday meal, or Sunday get together. If it is not made immediately the bone will be placed in a freezer bag, to use later. All you do is take one large slab of ham bone (with some meat left on) and boil it in a pot of water. After some time of brewing in the water the flavors of the bone permeate the entire pot of soup stock.

Later vegetables and other spices are added and you have the best homemade vegetable soup known to man. Serve it up with good ole' sweet cornbread, and butter, and it's finger licking good. If there is still more flavor left in the bone, it will once again be put in a freezer bag, and saved for another soup later. The question is then raised, "Well how do you know that there is more flavor in the bone?" That's easy, you just lick the bone and you will know if it still has flavor. Call the whole family up to the dinner table on a nice cold night, and chances are many will sit around for awhile, dipping over and over again back into the pot for more. The reason this meal works so well is because the bone has so much flavor in it both from the bone itself, and from the marrow. It serves as a bouillon cube, or broth and it's free, because you have it left over after one of your family meals. The south is about flavor, and many dishes have ham bone as a part of them. It's a real treat to have this meal, even if you did not grow up in the south. When you're done finally with the bone, give it to the dog.

The stories will be tied together at the end of the chapter, but for now let's move on to our next illustration. This is the story of another Ham, and this one is about Noah and his son Ham. Noah and his family have just survived the flood by God's providence, and the ark came to rest on land once again. This is where the story picks up.

The sons of Noah who went forth from the ark were Shem, Ham, and Japheth. (Ham was the father of Canaan.) These three were the sons of Noah, and from these the people of the whole earth were dispersed. Noah began to be a man of the soil, and he planted a vineyard. He drank of the wine and became drunk and lay uncovered in his tent. And Ham, the father of Canaan, saw the nakedness of his father and told his two brothers outside. Then Shem and Japheth took a garment, laid it on both their shoulders, and walked backward and covered the nakedness of their father. Their faces were turned backward, and they did not see their father's nakedness. When Noah awoke from his wine and knew what his youngest son had done to him, he said, "Cursed be Canaan; a servant of servants shall he be to his brothers." He also said, "Blessed be the LORD, the God of Shem; and let Canaan be his servant. May God enlarge Japheth, and let him dwell in the tents of Shem, and let Canaan be his servant.

Genesis 9:18-27

So in this story we see how Noah's son Ham responded incorrectly to his' father's moment of sin/weakness. Ham responded wrongly and his family took on a curse, and the other son's were blessed because of their appropriate response. A great verse that represents this story is found in: 1 Peter 4:8 "Above all, keep loving one another earnestly, since love covers a multitude of sins."

Moving on to my next illustration, I will talk about what I learned from a church conference I attended in Northern Minnesota. I was asked to work as a farm hand for a church in Minnesota and happily accepted the offer. In a season in my life when I was working as a missionary, I embraced the opportunity to attend conferences wherever I could. One night I was invited to a church to hear a guest speaker. As soon as I arrived, I became unsettled in my spirit. As soon as this man began to speak his arrogance flowed out of his mouth. Within 5 minutes I was ready to leave and head home.

Having ridden with someone in their vehicle I could not leave, so I was stuck! I literally tuned the guy out for most of what he said. But very gently the Lord started to work on my heart during that time, and I opened myself to listen better. By the end of his "painful" sermon, I heard one amazing nugget of truth. I had been speaking with God on another day about this particular nugget, that this speaker happened to also address. However this nugget the pastor gave really ministered to my soul and heart. It was truly a piece of meat from the Lord. If I would have been free to leave,

THE CALL FOR CHARACTER

or tuned this guy out, I would have missed an important opportunity for good meat. In this season, God showed me how to separate the "Meat from the Bones"!

God showed me the frailty of humanity and the truth that we all have some mixture of meat and bones in our lives. Some may be walking closer with the Lord, and they may give 80% good meat when they preach. Though they still have 20% bones that are man's thoughts. Other's like this pastor had 95% bones and one nugget of 5% meat. God was teaching me how to hear everyone out completely. As is stated in 1 Corinthians 14:29 "Let two or three prophets speak, and let the others weigh what is said." Jesus was the only human that was 100% meat all the time. Because God taught me this, I can now listen to any speaker more fully waiting to receive good meat, and gently discarding the bad bones. Truly it is a powerful thing to realize when we listen to other believers in a place of position, or platform.

After reading these past three illustrations it is now important to start tying these thoughts together. Here is the problem in the Body of Christ today; people do not know how to handle sin, and bones correctly. As with the case of Ham in the second story, he saw his "Righteous" father step into a place of failure. Instead of covering his father's shame, he went to reveal it to his brothers. Ham exposed and mocked his father's error, while his brother's acted and responded correctly, covering Noah honorably in his shame. Ham is an example of a subject, or follower who did not handle a sinful situation properly. Even though Ham saw it correctly for what it was, he did not respond correctly for what was needed.

An important attribute of a prophetic person is "Spiritual Eyesight". When God gives you a prophetic gift, he often gives a deeper discernment to see things. It is in these moments where you can choose to respond correctly or not. Ham had sight; he lacked insight. It is not enough to see but we must look deeper to understand what God is trying to show and impart.

The other problem of seeing things prophetically is that it attracts others to you who like to murmur or gossip. This is where the greatest classroom must be learned for you! If you have not already experienced what I am talking about here, I am sure you will soon enough. There are many today in the body of Christ that would rather murmur about a leader than to cover him when he errs. See the reality is that, ALL preachers have some portions of meat, and some of bones. It is not our duty to expose every bone to others around us. When God places in your heart this message of "Covering" you truly will toss the bone to the trash quickly. The people who want to bad mouth, or murmur about the bones of a preacher or minister are simply like dogs.

Dogs love to chew on a good "Ham Bone". Once the dog gets his bone, he will chew on it for awhile and lick the flavor. He then will go and bury it to save it to chew on at a later time of desire. Dogs love to chew on their bones full of flavor. And this is exactly what people do when they murmur, gossip, or bad mouth a leader. Pastor Larry Doe preaches his sermon and says one thing in the wrong tone, well the truth is, that's a bone. But now ten people in the congregation picked up the bone and they spend their entire Sunday afternoon chewing on it, and sucking the flavor from the bone. Pastor Larry loves the Lord and made a mistake, and he should be forgiven quickly if he made a small blunder from the platform. But just like the dogs, the people have saved a bone for their gossip at a later time.

The words of a gossip are like choice morsels as they descend to the innermost parts of the body.

Proverbs 18:8 (ISV)

Therefore because you are a prophetic person, and you can see things, sometimes it attracts gossips, and people who murmur, but you as a prophetic person need not give ear to any bone chewing. You must quickly identify these types of people, and draw safe boundaries so that you and your family do not get sucked into the snares of making "Spiritual Ham Bone Soup". Yet remember that those who gossip can be changed, and transformed into vessels of purity. Therefore, when you have the right chance to exhort them about their lips of destruction, please do so with utter care and tenderness. God desires everyone to be a healthy vessel, even those who need a swift rebuke about the tongue. If the gossips, never get exhorted correctly, then perhaps they will never change. A loving word of truth can go far in changing a deceptive word of destruction.

Another area of bone chewing that it is important to discuss is that of leadership when it speaks to you. Not all bone chewing happens only among the congregation, for there are many places where leaders speak to followers when they should not. If you are not an elder in a church, then in no way should an elder be speaking to you about the problems of other believers in that church. Nor should that elder speak to you about another elder's problems. We have all been in need of good leadership over us, and it will do us all well to remember, that leadership is above us who follow. Don't get taken into bone chewing conversations even if it gives you more chances to be with leadership. This is beyond words, one of the easiest traps with which you can fall. Leadership who chews on bones of members, and members who chew on the bones of leaders must be properly dealt with as the Scripture commands.

To further instruct us about covering sin and "bones" let's take a look at a few more scriptures before we continue.

Hatred stirreth up strifes: but love covereth all sins.

Proverbs 10:12 (KJV)

Whoever goes about slandering reveals secrets, but he who is trustworthy in spirit keeps a thing covered.

Proverbs 11:13

A fool's wrath is presently known: but a prudent man covereth shame.

Proverbs 12:16 (KJV)

To balance this equation correctly, it is now important to discuss the matter of exposing sin in a brief manner. Though love may cover a multitude of sins, this does not give room to turn a blind eye when someone is in error. Scripture does speak clearly about matters that we are able to see.

Take no part in the unfruitful works of darkness, but instead expose them. For it is shameful even to speak of the things that they do in secret. But when anything is exposed by the light, it becomes visible, for anything that becomes visible is light. Therefore it says, "Awake, O sleeper, and arise from the dead, and Christ will shine on you." Look carefully then how you walk, not as unwise but as wise, making the best use of the time, because the days are evil.

Ephesians 5:11-16

In the situation of Ham, he would have done well to have covered his father, and spoken to him privately later after his drunken stupor wore off. Though as we see he did not, and it revealed the heart behind his actions. Scripture tells us in the New Testament clearly how to deal with matters of sin. These commands and the proper order show us there is a time and a place to confront a brother in sin. However these are all done privately at first, and not spoken of to others in way of gossiping.

It is very important to follow scripture when it comes to confronting a sin issue with someone else. If your heart is right, then you will walk in utter tenderness in dealing with the sin.

There are those however who see sin, and arrogantly expose it leaving all parties affected naked and uncovered for all to see. These people do not demonstrate the heart of love and redemption behind such speaking. God always desires redemption for sinners and pure restoration. If someone comes in on a "Crusaders Horse" to confront a matter without love, then they place themselves above God's order and chosen authority. God wants mercy. Look at what he did with the woman caught in adultery! He bent over and started writing in the sand, and I genuinely believe as do many, this was to get the eyesight off of her nakedness. Just because someone see's the problem does not give them the right to address it. Furthermore when they address it, they better be filled with love, and redemption. This is not a ministry of ripping the skirt off of pagans in their debauchery, but a ministry of clothing the believers who are in sin.

Listen friends, if you see a brother in sin and you know God has given you the task to confront the matter, first and foremost cover his nakedness. Then when the time is right, go to him and speak to the matter of sin privately. In that, you demonstrate both justice, and love in the process. If we don't give mercy to others then we elect ourselves as judges over them. Mercy always triumphs over judgment!

If there is a time when you do not know what to do in a situation about sin, I suggest you pray, and ask the Lord to guide you. It is also right to seek the advice of a pure leader or trusted mature friend in the Lord. There are many situations like some that have already been mentioned where the advice may or may not be right. This is why it is always best to walk in true communion with the Holy Spirit, for his confirmation in each of these matters. You will not be left to make your own choices because God will show you the right way to handle it, if you listen!

It is greatly important for us to practice tossing bones away and covering sin as quickly as possible. Let there be no shame to a leader who speaks and sometimes gives you a bone. Man is man, and is totally fallible in his ways. We all make mistakes; there is no one perfect except Jesus. We will do well to give grace to speakers and leaders when they preach; they are there to build us up. If you have been storing bones to use against other brothers or sisters, it is due time for you to spit them out and clean house. There is no room in God's ministry for bone chewing, or for scoffing, gossiping, or murmuring. Bones have flavor not spiritual nutrients. You cannot be sustained on the flavor of bones. The reason people chew on bones full of flavor is because they have lost or neglected the flavor of the

Lord in their mouth. We are the salt of the earth, and we have all the flavor we need in Jesus. If you do not have salt in your life, return to the Lord, and to his Word.

In conclusion, guarding your tongue from this type of danger will greatly benefit your prophetic journey. Even those who are not called prophetically, will do well to learn this encouragement as well. We are to anoint our tongue with the Holy Spirit, as well as love and redemption, not with the flavor of death and destruction. No matter how much it may taste to your likings you must not partake of this forbidden fruit. To maintain an anointed tongue, means that your prophetic diet will differ from that of those who walk around you. Eat the meat, spit out the bones, and cover sin carefully.

CHAPTER NINE

Pour Me Sweet Water

If you spend your life chewing on the bones and flaws of other people, chances are you will inherit bitterness. The truest outcome of bone chewing produces this bitterness and eventually cursing. In this chapter I will talk about the bitterness, and in Chapter Ten I will go into detail more about the cursing. There will be a very similar essence to both of these topics in Nine and Ten. But in this chapter we will focus on how bitterness creeps in to your life, and the solution to solving this problem. If you are a seer, or prophetic person you will deal with bitterness. It's not about if it comes, but when it comes, and how you respond to it, both in yourself and in others. A prophet must be flowing of sweet water, are you thirsty?

First let's define the word bitter and bitterness; then I will discuss a few Biblical accounts that reveal bitterness.

Bitter as Defined in Webster's... "Sharp, or biting to the taste; acrid; like wormwood. Sharp; cruel; severe; as bitter enmity. Sharp, as words, reproachful; sarcastic. Sharp to the feeling; piercing; painful; that makes to smart; as a bitter cold day, or a bitter blast. Painful to the mind; calamitous; poignant; as a bitter fate. Afflicted; distressed. Hurtful; very sinful."

Bitter From Brown-Driver-Briggs Hebrew... "A drop flowing down, a trickle, to make bitter, of food, cry, pain, a harlots end, to be enraged."

The heart knows its own bitterness, and no stranger shares its joy.

Proverbs 14:10

See to it that no one fails to obtain the grace of God; that no "root of bitterness" springs up and causes trouble, and by it many become defiled

Hebrews 12:15

We all know what bitterness looks like. Identifying bitterness is often an easy task. But often we don't know when it has taken a hold of us. This is the case with the first story about Jonah. Jonah was given an assignment by the Lord to preach to Ninevah, (The capital of Israel's hated enemies). Jonah refused to go to Ninevah, but after whale persuasion and a heart change, Jonah yielded to the heart of the Lord and obeyed God by going and preaching to Ninevah.

The people of Ninevah were very terrible, and easy to dislike for good reasons. This is where we will pick up our story with Jonah.

Then the word of the LORD came to Jonah the second time, saying, "Arise, go to Nineveh, that great city, and call out against it the message that I tell you." So Jonah arose and went to Nineveh, according to the word of the LORD. Now Nineveh was an exceedingly great city, three days' journey in breadth. Jonah began to go into the city, going a day's journey. And he called out, "Yet forty days, and Nineveh shall be overthrown!" And the people of Nineveh believed God. They called for a fast and put on sackcloth, from the greatest of them to the least of them. The word reached the king of Nineveh, and he arose from his throne, removed his robe, covered himself with sackcloth, and sat in ashes. And he issued a proclamation and published through Nineveh, "By the decree of the king and his nobles: Let neither man nor beast, herd nor flock, taste anything. Let them not feed or drink water, but let man and beast be covered with sackcloth, and let them call out mightily to God. Let everyone turn from his evil way and from the violence that is in his hands. Who knows? God may turn and relent and turn from his fierce anger, so that we may not perish." When God saw what they did, how they turned from their evil way, God relented of the disaster that he had said he would do to them, and he did not do it.

Jonah Chapter 3

But it displeased Jonah exceedingly, and he was angry. And he prayed to the LORD and said, "O LORD, is not this what I said when I was yet in my country? That is why I made haste to flee to Tarshish; for I knew that you are a gracious God and merciful, slow to anger and abounding in steadfast love, and relenting from disaster. Therefore now, O LORD, please take my life from me, for it is better for me to die than to live." And the LORD said, "Do you do well to be angry?

Jonah Chapter 4: 1-4

So it is easy to see that Jonah got bitter, and actually went to pout outside the city. The discourse between God and Jonah is very valuable to read, and I encourage it. What was incredibly peculiar was that Jonah was angry that the Ninevites repented from their sins, and turned to the Lord. Perhaps Jonah's bitterness took such a hold onto his life, he could not even rejoice when these lost pagans were rescued from the wrath of the Lord. No mistake can be made when you read this passage that Jonah was bitter and angry for this turn of events. One would think this prophet would rejoice with the Lord in the streets for their salvation.

Jonah's circumstances caused him to be bitter, and most likely he fed that bitterness to such a point of no personal victory. For the next story about bitterness let's go to one of the best examples of bitterness in a people. This is the story of Marah.

Can you imagine that the children of Israel just got freed from Egypt by great and awesome miracles of the Lord? Then they were led by fire and a cloud to the Red Sea, to see it miraculously parted and the entire Egyptian army swallowed up. With great songs they broke out praising the Lord for his mighty deliverance and victories. It was then only 3 days later where they found themselves without water in the wilderness. Then they came upon the waters of Marah. Here is where we will pick up the story.

> *Then Miriam the prophetess, Aaron's sister, took a tambourine in her hand and went out with all the women behind her with tambourines and dancing. Miriam sang to them, "Sing to the LORD, for he is highly exalted! The horse and its rider he has thrown into the sea." Then Moses led Israel from the Reed Sea and they went to the desert of Shur. They traveled into the desert for three days and did not find water. When they came to Marah, they could not drink the water at Marah because it was bitter. (That is why it's called Marah.) Then the people complained against Moses: "What are we to drink?" Moses cried out to the LORD, and the LORD showed him a tree, which he threw into the water, and the water became sweet. There the LORD presented to them a statute and an ordinance, and there he tested them. He said, "If you will carefully obey the LORD your God, do what is right in his eyes, listen to his commandments, and keep all his statutes, then I won't inflict on you all the diseases that I inflicted on the Egyptians, because I am the LORD your healer." Then they came to Elim where there were twelve springs of water and 70 palm trees, and they camped there by the water.*
>
> *Exodus 15:20-27*

How incredibly amazing is the reality of this passage! As was just said, the children saw God do mighty miracles. Three days later they were murmuring and had bitterness. "Where is our water?" Isn't it interesting to see how quickly the Lord tested his people after seeing great victories. Now this passage is not exactly revealing the life of a prophet, but we can draw great comparisons and truths from it, to examine the fruit of bitterness. It is also interesting to realize that there is a large possibility that the waters of Marah, represented symbolically what was in the people's hearts.

So by looking at these first two scenarios we can gather that bitterness can come rapidly, and easily to anyone's life. The question then raised is, "What is the solution to bitterness?" The clearest answer is found in this previous story.

"What are we to drink?" Moses cried out to the LORD, and the LORD showed him a tree, which he threw into the water, and the water became sweet."

There is no doubt this tree is a reference to the cross of Jesus Christ, and because of this example it is the answer for us even today. When Jesus DAILY pours his Spirit into our lives we are kept free of bitter waters. If we leave any time gap between our pure fellowship with Him, there is a chance our circumstances will cause us to turn bitter. The reason why bitterness creeps in so quickly is easy to understand. Because you can see and discern things, it is easy to see many of the problems around you prophetically. This is exactly what happened to Jonah. He saw the problem, got angry at the sin, and became bitter towards the people. Potentially it is fair to say that Jonah might have preferred judgment rather than mercy on those terrible people. God came to Jonah and taught him symbolically through another tree how good mercy feels. Oh how tender the Lord is with his children!

Bitterness trickles in so easily to the body, that over time you might not even catch yourself speaking bitterly about people or situations. If you do catch yourself, the only solution is to throw the cross into your well. Jesus intends for us to pour out sweet water to others, and if we are walking in bitterness we cannot. You may not choose the circumstances in your life, and you may get placed in very hard, difficult, and wretched places. But you can choose whether you will stay bitter or not.

If you allow the waters of your life to be muddied by bitterness you will not be able to see, discern, or respond to a situation correctly. So before you speak to a matter, allow God to sift out the mud, and purify your waters so you can once again see with clarity. Then and only then, will you be able to speak and give sweet water. If you don't have a cup of sweet water to pour out, get alone with God until your well runs sweetly clear.

Once you are running clear with sweet water, you can begin to pour out words of redemption and restoration. You can also identify those who are not running clear, and who are walking in bitterness. Seeing bitterness in someone else is a very delicate matter. You can see it in their eyes, hear it in their mouths, and see it in their actions.

While these people who walk in bitterness are dangerous, they are not enemies if they are believers. Just like we saw in the Webster's definition these people who walk in bitterness are "Afflicted and Distressed". These people are bound by bitterness and stuck in its bondage, and they too need freedom. While they may be a loose cannon and bearing bad fruit, God still desires that even these find redemption and pure water.

We must be willing to come along side of bitter people "briefly" to bring to their attention their root of bitterness. We should be extremely careful that we do not take on their bitterness, but this does not stop us from reaching out to them in their affliction. Jesus demonstrated this well with the man who had been sick for 40 years, and was bitter. This too is an example to us how to reach out to someone who is bitter. This man lying by the pool of Solomon's porch, was bitter because no one helped him into the water to get well, and others got there first. He was completely bitter at everyone, yet Jesus went down to him, and restored him. The cross life of Jesus was "dipped" into that man, and he was healed completely. So we too need to recognize others who need a touch like this and give it to them. If we don't take heart, to reach out to these people, bitterness will bring them down a road of destruction.

A true prophet does not only see, he also feels, as was stated in The Prophetic Sigh chapter. Sometimes seeing things so heinous can cause us to become grief stricken to the point that we end up eating the fruit of bitterness. This bitterness can cause us to look at a person in their sin-like state and say "It is impossible", causing us to desire destruction in their lives rather than deliverance and redemption. But this cannot be so. We must get out from under that "lonely tree of resentment" and ask the Lord to put life back into our being, so we can once again speak life into other human beings. No matter how bad the situation may seem God can breathe upon it and bring life. There are so many times as prophetic people that we can become disgusted with the things we see and turn inward, removing ourselves from the wretchedness of mankind. But this removal from others is not the heart of God. For the final two accounts let's take a look at the life of Paul and Jesus.

> *I am speaking the truth in Christ—I am not lying; my conscience bears me witness in the Holy Spirit that I have great sorrow and unceasing anguish in my heart. For I could wish that I myself were accursed and cut off from Christ for the sake of my brothers, my kinsmen according to the flesh.*
>
> *Romans 9:1-3*

In this passage we have Paul speaking of the Jews. These were the very ones who rejected him and the gospel of Jesus. They were known to mock him, beat him, and severely persecute him. Because of this Paul had a great reason to harbor bitterness. Yet Paul shows ultimately the heart of Jesus in this passage. He wishes himself accursed for their sake.

What Paul is saying here is that he would rather receive "Damnation" and "Separation" from Christ if only he could see the Jews come to salvation. This is a brother who has had a revelation of the Cross, and has constantly been dipping that cross into the waters of his heart. There is no way a bitter heart could produce such a generous and unselfish statement like his. Paul had totally restrained himself from taking on bitterness towards the very people that Jesus sent him to. We as prophetic people need a constant revealing of the cross to our hearts. If we behold the sacrifice of Christ for sinners, then we will have no problem staying out of bitterness.

Now when we look at Jesus we see that he was a man of sorrow and grief. His heart broke when he saw the state of mankind. In that brokenness he chose to leave his perfect abode in heaven, to become a man on earth, so that he could save mankind from their sins. Looking at the life of Jesus we can most certainly see that if anyone had a right to be bitter it was him. Think about it: The creator was rejected by the very ones he created, and the very one who defined love was denied the love of his people. But in all of this he did not become bitter.

In the Garden of Gethsemane, he could have said, "Why should I die for these ungrateful people?" But instead he said, "Father not my will be done, but yours!" So we have seen that Paul wished himself accursed for the sake of the brethren. We also see that Jesus wished himself accursed for his people, by becoming that curse. But how did he do it? The Cross… the cross was always in the heart of Jesus, for he was slain before the foundations of the world, and in that cross, was, and is, the redemption for mankind. With a mission like that, bitterness could not be allowed to creep in.

We as prophets must also have the mission of redemption. If we can look forward, past people's present state and see the redemption of the cross in their lives, we will not partake of that "Bitter Fruit" that so easily creeps into our lives. There will be many times on this journey, we will find opportunities to become bitter towards the lost, and even other believers. But God is looking for people who will pull others out of the mire instead of throwing them into the fire.

To love people that love you is easy, for even the world does that. But to love others that hate and despise you, comes from the love Christ shows toward us. He laid down his life for us when we didn't deserve it, and we are called to do the same. Not only must we have a "Dipping" of the Cross in our hearts and lives, but there also needs to be a remaining of that cross especially in those places that we can become easily bitter. If our hearts stay cross centered we will do well and speak correctly.

Doth a fountain send forth at the same place sweet water and bitter?
James 3:11 (KJV)

The only question remains, what does your fountain taste like?

CHAPTER TEN

Blessings & Cursing–The Tongue of the Prophet

If your fountain is pouring forth bitter water, then eventually your mouth will pour forth cursing, and destruction. A good illustration of this would be to compare bitter water as gasoline, and sweet water as purified water. Let's take two plants and water them for 3 weeks using these two elements: gasoline and purified water. Over the next 3 weeks (sometimes overnight) you will notice the plant with gasoline as its water will turn brown, shrivel up, and die. While the plant that received nutrients from the purified water, received life, and growth from its soil. There is no way to reverse the effects of gasoline on a plant, it can only die as an end result. However, sometimes if caught early on it could be reversed, but in the long run much damage will have been caused, and the plant will suffer greatly. This is the clear reality of our choice to bless or curse with our tongue.

Throughout the entire course of Scripture, God has laid before us the reality of choice. We have not been made as robots; we have been made with a free will to choose. The love of God and his mercy gives us the choice to choose His ways or ours. Here is one of the first examples of this in the Old Testament.

> *I call heaven and earth to record this day against you, that I have set before you life and death, blessing and cursing: therefore choose life, that both thou and thy seed may live: That thou mayest love the LORD thy God, and that thou mayest obey his voice, and that thou mayest cleave unto him: for he is thy life, and the length of thy days: that thou mayest dwell in the land which the LORD sware unto thy fathers, to Abraham, to Isaac, and to Jacob, to give them.*
>
> *Deuteronomy 30:19-20 (KJV)*

The children of Israel were close to reaching the promised land, and crossing over into it. Moses here was an oracle of God, and spoke God's heart clearly out before the people. The heart of God is simple, he wanted them to choose Him at all times, and not any other idols. If they chose God, they would be blessed, and if they rejected Him they would be cursed. This is a beautiful comparison to the choices of our tongue. Throughout Scripture God instructs us about this choice and what He desires for us to do. Here are a few more verses about this choice.

> *...But the tongue can no man tame; it is an unruly evil, full of deadly poison. Therewith bless we God, even the Father; and therewith curse we men, which are made after the similitude of God. Out of the same mouth proceedeth blessing and cursing. My brethren, these things ought not so to be.*
>
> *James 3:8-10(KJV)*

There is one whose rash words are like sword thrusts, but the tongue of the wise brings healing.

Proverbs 12:18

Death and life are in the power of the tongue, and those who love it will eat its fruits.

Proverbs 18:21

A gentle tongue is a tree of life, but perverseness in it breaks the spirit.

Proverbs 15:4

Bless those who persecute you; bless and do not curse them.

Romans 12:14

...But I say to you who hear, Love your enemies, do good to those who hate you, bless those who curse you, pray for those who abuse you.

Luke 6:27-28

...But I say unto you, Love your enemies, bless them that curse you, do good to them that hate you, and pray for them which despitefully use you, and persecute you.

Matthew 5:44

Throughout Scripture we hear from inspired prophets, kings, and even Jesus himself about the reality of blessing others. There is no mistake in scripture that God's heart is to bless first not curse. This same heart needs to come into our Spirit when we approach prophetic ministry. Why? Because we are in the "Age of Grace", and Jesus Christ is seated on the "Mercy

Seat" with his arms open wide to save people from their sins. As long as we are in this Age of Grace we as believers should be walking with the heart of blessing toward others. Let's take a deeper look now at the Season of Grace and what it means to us, and the ministry God has called us to.

> *For God so loved the world, that he gave his only Son, that whoever believes in him should not perish but have eternal life. For God did not send his Son into the world to condemn the world, but in order that the world might be saved through him.*

> *Whoever believes in him is not condemned, but whoever does not believe is condemned already, because he has not believed in the name of the only Son of God. And this is the judgment: the light has come into the world, and people loved the darkness rather than the light because their works were evil.*

> *John 3:16-19*

This was the ministry of Jesus during his first coming on the earth, to save. He came to send out the call of salvation as a free gift, and this call will go forth until he returns the second time. This is what will happen when He returns the second time.

> *"Then I saw heaven opened, and behold, a white horse! The one sitting on it is called Faithful and True, and in righteousness he judges and makes war. His eyes are like a flame of fire, and on his head are many diadems, and he has a name written that no one knows but himself. He is clothed in a robe dipped in blood, and the name by which he is called is The Word of God. And the armies of heaven, arrayed in fine linen, white and pure, were following him*

on white horses. From his mouth comes a sharp sword with which to strike down the nations, and he will rule them with a rod of iron. He will tread the winepress of the fury of the wrath of God the Almighty. On his robe and on his thigh he has a name written, King of kings and Lord of lords."

Revelation 19:11-16

If we are to walk and talk as God's prophets we must see God as a God of mercy, and we must understand and know what Season we are walking in. We are walking in the Age of Grace. As the people of God we must be "Warning" men to flee from the coming judgment, and we should not be "Pointing" them, neither sending them to that judgment. Seeing Jesus on that throne of mercy will cause us to instruct such rebels to turn from God's wrath and run into his refuge of Love. In regards to wickedness and darkness our job is not to turn a blind eye. Rather we need to shine the light of God's truth, and we are not to curse them with a judgment. Jesus came into this world not to condemn it, but to save it. Our hearts must desire to see men come to salvation and not damnation. God has no desire that the cursed should remain cursed, but if we shine the light on men's dark deeds and they do not repent, they pronounce judgment on themselves.

In regards to God's throne of Judgment, God is only sentencing individuals to the judgment that they have already pronounced on themselves through unbelief. God is long-suffering towards all of us, and is giving us opportunity to repent.

In rebellion towards God's mercy, wicked people do not realize that once God gets off that throne of mercy, to sit on the throne of Judgment, there is no longer mercy towards the unbeliever.

This time has not come yet, and while Jesus remains in that mercy seat we are to be speaking forth the blessings of God, and not the curses. When we begin to curse and walk out from underneath that umbrella of mercy we replace our titles as, "Ministers of Mercy" and become "Juror's of Judgment". These jurors are those that pronounce judgment and destruction on people, yet they never claim or reclaim any lives for the kingdom of God.

The reason why I speak on this topic so emphatically is because there are MANY prophetic loose cannons in the body of Christ right now. There are many who think they should call down fire from heaven on sinners, while others may wish for people to be consumed in illness or death. The sad reality is, there are many who think it is ok to pray this way toward others. The heart of God does not delight in the death of the unrighteous as we have already seen. The call to repentance is sent forth and the free gift of salvation is waiting for those who want to take it. This is the same theme and tone that we should be speaking in, always to the lost. This is clearly visible in how Jesus responded to his disciples after their response to rejection.

> And it came to pass, when the time was come that he should be received up, he steadfastly set his face to go to Jerusalem, And sent messengers before his face: and they went, and entered into a village of the Samaritans, to make ready for him. And they did not receive him, because his face was as though he would go to Jerusalem. And when his disciples James and John saw this, they said, Lord, wilt thou that we command fire to come down from heaven, and consume them, even as Elias did? But he turned, and rebuked them, and said, Ye know not what manner of spirit ye are of. For the Son of man is not come to destroy men's lives, but to save them. And they went to another village.
>
> *Luke 9:51-56 (KJV)*

Here the disciples stepped out of their place walking with the King of Mercy, and took on the role of Judge in an Old Covenant manifestation.

How many times have we thought or prayed the same way as the disciples?

If we are not careful we will step in into a ministry that God never intended. Many young prophets today see the Prophets of Old, and want to do the same things as they did, but we are in a different covenant today. I would be lying if I said that I hadn't thought this way in my infant Christian years as well. But praise the Lord he reveals his heart of redemption and mercy to us all. In the Christian community there are many different camps of thinking about prophetic ministry, but the heart of God is manifesting in the New Covenant.

Some people see the ministry of Elijah as their personal destiny in life, but this may have potential dangers if approached in the wrong spirit. I have heard many people reference the ministry of the "Two Witnesses" in Revelation, and assume that their ministry can use the same dynamics. The ministry of the Two Witnesses whether literal or symbolic is a ministry given to them by God for a specific season and purpose. This is not that season. Yet, many see the calling of the witnesses and wish to perform their ministry also. To that I say emphatically, 99.9999999999% of you are not them, nor am I. Therefore we should not presume to walk in a place that is not ours to have. We are ministers of mercy, not judgment. Furthermore their ministry is actually a ministry of mercy through afflictions, but still it is God given to them, not us.

We can walk in the wrong Spirit sometimes, just like the disciples did if we do not remain in the mercy of the Lord. Jesus rebuked them for being in the wrong spirit, and reminded them what his true purpose was. If we listen correctly to the heart beat of Jesus we will be careful what we say. Remember, we are saving them from the mire not throwing them into the fire.

We can however walk in the right spirit and still pray prayers of violence on the kingdom of darkness. In this process the prayers of the heart should never be for the destruction of life, but for redemption. The entire foundation of any prayer like this starts in the heart of redemption and restoration. If you cannot in your whole conscience pray a prayer seeing redemption in mind, there is a large chance your prayer has an essence of cursing on it. So we don't get confused, there is a drastic difference between pronouncing judgments on people, as opposed to speaking curses over people. This is not a topic about pronouncing judgments, but it is being stated clearly that we should not curse people with our tongues. We need to be preaching repentance not speaking forth curses.

If you are cursing someone, for the sake of cursing, and you get excitement off of that destruction, you are indeed in the wrong spirit. A really good example of the right heart attitude towards enemies is that of David and his persecutors. In this situation David prayed that God would not destroy them, and therefore reveals the heart of redemption. We too must pray for those who persecute us, in the same manner. Whether you are responding to persecution, a person in sin, or a fellow believer we must not speak with curses towards that person, and must see the potential treasure in them. The goal is not to clear the earth of its sinners, but to redeem a people wandering without the knowledge of God.

Again I wish to say emphatically that the heart of your prayers must reflect the heart of the Father, and his heart wants to see life in people, not death on any level. The types of prayers that wreak havoc on the kingdom of darkness are prayers that come against strongholds. Let's look at what scripture says about the battle we fight.

> Put on the whole armour of God, that ye may be able to stand against the wiles of the devil. For we wrestle not against flesh and blood, but against principalities, against powers, against the rulers of the darkness of this world, against spiritual wickedness in high places. Wherefore take unto you the whole armour of God, that ye may be able to withstand in the evil day, and having done all, to stand.
>
> Ephesians 6:11-13 (KJV)

To illustrate how this is appropriate warfare, let's take the example of a bar or strip club in your neighborhood. It would be totally appropriate to pray against that facility, to see it close and no longer function for evil. It would not be appropriate to pray for it to be destroyed and lives lost in the process. However tearing down high places in the "Spiritual Domain" is always appropriate. In the Old Testament the act of tearing down a High Place was totally appropriate and seen as very righteous. However today in our current society of high standards and morals, we are bound to laws that are more detailed and enforced against such actions. If you go and burn a building with your hands, this is a problem. Today this will be considered as "Vandalism", and we cannot do this. We MUST walk and war in the "Spiritual" and not in the "Physical". This reveals the problem for us in this prophetic classroom. You may, and indeed we do have the hearts of Old Testament prophets, though we are bound by love to walk out the New Covenant as given by Jesus.

> *For though we walk in the flesh, we are not waging war according to the flesh. For the weapons of our warfare are not of the flesh but have divine power to destroy strongholds.*
>
> *2 Corinthians 10:3-4*

It boils down to two choices in your ministry; you can either bless someone, or you can curse someone. If both of these are valid options, we better have the mind of the Lord in doing it. My personal opinion is this; that if error be made, I would rather error by blessing all the time instead of taking the liberty to curse or condemn. This can be made visible when you compare the story of Ichabod, and Ezekiel. The heart behind these two portions of scripture can be boiled down to two choices of speech.

In the case of Ichabod, we can see that the Priesthood was in utter failure, the son's of the priest were in horrible sin, and the people were in destruction. At the time of Eli it looked horrible, bleak, and without hope. His sons were running around in rampant sin, debauchery, and destruction. Eli's prophetic fervor and spiritual backbone was gone, and the children of the Lord were without a good shepherd. Eli's daughter was horribly plagued by the circumstances, and therefore looking at the whole matter named her baby out of a heart of hopelessness and cursing. She yelled

ICHABOD and that means, "The Glory of God has Departed". This is easy for anyone to do in their situations. The scenario you or I are in may look horrible, but we must remain steadfast, and hold to the hope in Jesus for redemption. We must not be quick to curse a matter to desolation.

In the other account we see Ezekiel, come upon a hopeless situation, and the Lord came to him with a question. "Do you think these bones can live?" It's amazing to see a valley full of death, bones, and desolation! What horror, and hopeless that must have felt like. Yet Ezekiel asked God to reveal his heart, and He did. "Speak to the bones that they may live!" So Ezekiel went beyond his eyesight of hopelessness, and embraced God's heart of Tenderness! God wanted the dead bones to live, and Ezekiel was obedient and spoke that message of Blessings and Life. He yelled, "Dry Bones LIVE!!!"

In conclusion to this chapter I would like to end with being redundant again! We have been given two choices from God when we speak. We can choose blessings or cursing.

> *Bless those who persecute you; bless and do not curse them. Rejoice with those who rejoice, weep with those who weep. Live in harmony with one another. Do not be haughty, but associate with the lowly. Never be wise in your own sight. Repay no one evil for evil, but give thought to do what is honorable in the sight of all. If possible, so far as it depends on you, live peaceably with all. Beloved, never avenge yourselves, but leave it to the wrath of God, for it is written, "Vengeance is mine, I will repay, says the Lord." To the contrary, "if your enemy is hungry, feed him; if he is thirsty, give him something to drink; for by so doing you will heap burning coals on his head." Do not be overcome by evil, but overcome evil with good.*
>
> *Romans 12:14-21*

Our heart must bear God's heart in the manifestation of our tongue. This is one of the biggest areas that our tongue needs to be anointed in. People will do us wrong because of the dark system at work around us. We must not be surprised by this. We will be hated, persecuted, slandered, and spoken evil of, but we must not retaliate with a curse. Jesus clearly rebuked the disciples for that wrong Spirit. Even if someone is a horrible, disgusting, crude, evil, vile, pagan, you should delight in praying for that person to be redeemed. As long as that person has breath, they have the chance to receive the free gift of salvation and repent. But if your heart is to slash and burn them in their sin, you are walking in the wrong Spirit. Jesus came for the sick, not for the healthy, and most are totally sick today.

The victory comes when the person is redeemed, and often that is in ways we least expect. God is so long-suffering, and will wait for a long time before He acts in judgment. So we too must carry the heart burden of God correctly. Therefore take heed to how you speak, and what outcome you desire to see. God's desire is that none shall perish, do we remember this?

> *With it we bless our Lord and Father, and with it we curse people who are made in the likeness of God. From the same mouth come blessing and cursing. My brothers, these things ought not to be so.*
>
> *James 3:9-10*

Does your heart desire to see sinner's repent, be restored, and LIVE? If you want a slash and burn ministry, you have picked the wrong Religion, for the Son of Man came not to destroy men's lives but save them!

CHAPTER ELEVEN

No Debates for the Prophet

Another important caution that is necessary to discuss for prophetic ministry, is that of having debates. If you want to walk with an anointed tongue it is important to clearly state that you cannot have the spirit of debate. In this chapter I would like to discuss my personal views on why The Christian person should not participate in conversations that are fueled by debate or quarreling. Saying this, it is important to point out the difference between debate, and discussion. However most people in our society see debates as approved intellectual arguments. My case is that this type of debating is not scripturally recognized as good. If however the voice of reason is present in a conversation, there can be a healthy discussion on a matter. But steer clear if you see arguments appear, for there should be No Debates for the Prophet!

First let's take a look at the definitions and terms that are important for this topic.

Debate (From Webster's)... "Contention in words or arguments; discussion for elucidating truth; strife in argument or reasoning, between persons of different opinions, each endeavoring to prove his own opinion right, and that of his opposer wrong; dispute; controversy; as the debates in parliament or in congress. Strife; contention. To engage in combat."

Debate (From Strong's)

"ERIS"   -   Quarrel, debate, strife, wrangling.

"REEB"   -   Grapple, wrangle, hold controversy.

"MATSTSAH"   -   Quarrel, contention, strife.

There is a large connection in these defining terms of debate and strife. Therefore it is necessary to also include strife's definitions and Greek terms, so that we can see how close and interchangeable these words are. In this passage from Romans 1:29 , the King James uses the word "Debate, while others use "Strife". But the Greek and Hebrew connections are clearly the same in the other passages in the Bible as well.

Even as they did not like to retain God in their knowledge, God gave them over to a reprobate mind, to do those things which are not convenient; Being filled with all unrighteousness, fornication, wickedness, covetousness, maliciousness; full of envy, murder, debate, deceit, malignity; whisperers,

Romans 1:28-29 KJV

Strife

Greek Definitions

G2054 – ERIS   -   Contention, strife, wrangling.

G2052–ERITHEIA   -   Electioneering, or intriguing for office

G485 – ANTIOLOGIA - Gainsaying, opposition, rebellion.

Hebrew Definitions

H7378–RUB   - To contend, to quarrel, with words also.

H7379 – RIB   - Controversy, dispute, at law also.

Vine's–Strife and contention, is the expression of enmity. Factions or contentions, fighting, disputes, and strife of words.

Webster's–Violent or bitter conflict or enmity, a struggle, a competition, rivalry.

Webster's 1828–Exertion or contention for superiority; contest of emulation, either by intellectual or physical efforts.

King James Bible–Romans 1:29 defines the word strife G2054 as debate.

Now that we have the main terms and definitions of Debate/Strife, let's move on to talk about what society thinks about debates. If you have ever been on a college campus in Europe or America, you will know how powerful this topic actually is for them. Because our students are taught to debate with the precision of a lawyer and intellectual prowess in any topic they select. Whether the students are Christians or not doesn't matter, because the University and College campuses are used to facilitate debates. The reality is they are not facilitating debates, as much as they are facilitating "Questioning". There is a whole other spirit behind this, and that spirit both wants to question truth, and cause debating about it. This is why the student is forced into an argumentative spirit even before they know it.

In this day we live in a society of intellectual giants who hide behind their lofty words, and eloquent speech. Such giants put fear in others, because of their ability to chew up and spit out, anyone who dares to challenge their intellect. People see this and desire to be just like them.

We as a society have become as the Greeks and seek after worldly wisdom, and relish in hearing enchanting words. We have numerous well educated people writing books, giving seminars, and forming debates so that they can, state their cause and prove their point, for the sake of being the superior one. Sadly such a mentality has crept into the church and the Spirit of Debate is being bred among the children of God.

In regards to the topic of debating, it is very important to say in a positive light that there is nothing wrong with a good "Question and Answer" session, as is in the case with much of Ravi Zacharias Ministries. However there is a fine line between a question that leads one to know truth, versus a question that leads one to an argument. Many studies have shown us that there are only two options in this matter: You either have a "Spirit of Debate", or you have a "Voice of Reason". A person who wants to reason, will be tempered and meek, but a person with a debating spirit will be untempered and arrogant. People are so unaware that there is an evil "Spirit of Debate" at work among many modern conversations. However even the Greeks knew this spirit at work, and I wish to Quote Matthew Clarke on this matter. "Debate, contention discord, etc... of this vile passion the Greeks made a goddess..."

To really understand the nature of debating, we need to see it in light of what it really is. Webster defines it best by saying, "endeavoring to prove his own opinion right, and that of his opposer wrong;. And with the definition of strife... "Exertion or contention for superiority." This is why debating for Christians is really not what the Word of God teaches. Let's examine several scripture verses that reference debating, in its true character.

> *And even as they did not like to retain God in their knowledge, God gave them over to a reprobate mind, to do those things which are not convenient; Being filled with all unrighteousness, fornication, wickedness, covetousness, maliciousness; full of envy, murder, debate, deceit, malignity; whisperers,.*
>
> *Romans 1:28-29 (KJV)*

Flee also youthful lusts: but follow righteousness, faith, charity, peace, with them that call on the Lord out of a pure heart. But foolish and unlearned questions avoid, knowing that they do gender strifes.

And the servant of the Lord must not strive; but be gentle unto all men, apt to teach, patient, In meekness instructing those that oppose themselves; if God peradventure will give them repentance to the acknowledging of the truth; And that they may recover themselves out of the snare of the devil, who are taken captive by him at his will.

2 Timothy 2:22-26 (KJV)

If any man teach otherwise, and consent not to wholesome words, even the words of our Lord Jesus Christ, and to the doctrine which is according to godliness; He is proud, knowing nothing, but doting about questions and strifes of words, whereof cometh envy, strife, railings, evil surmisings, perverse disputings of men of corrupt minds, and destitute of the truth, supposing that gain is godliness: from such withdraw thyself.

1 Timothy 6:3-5 (KJV)

As for the one who is weak in faith, welcome him, but not to quarrel over opinions.

Romans 14:1

But avoid foolish controversies, genealogies, dissensions, and quarrels about the law, for they are unprofitable and worthless. As for a person who stirs up division, after warning him once and then twice, have nothing more to do with him, knowing that such a person is warped and sinful; he is self-condemned.

Titus 3:9-11

But if ye have bitter envying and strife in your hearts, glory not, and lie not against the truth. This wisdom descendeth not from above, but is earthly, sensual, devilish. For where envying and strife is, there is confusion and every evil work. But the wisdom that is from above is first pure, then peaceable, gentle, and easy to be entreated, full of mercy and good fruits, without partiality, and without hypocrisy. And the fruit of righteousness is sown in peace of them that make peace.

James 3:14-18 (KJV)

Whoever meddles in a quarrel not his own is like one who takes a passing dog by the ears.

Proverbs 26:17

The Bible is clear about debating, and it categorizes it in with fleshly, and carnal manifestations. As prophets we cannot look toward our intellect to speak God's truth. If we begin to depend on how smart we are and speak out mere knowledge we are in danger of making the word of God of no effect. We are to walk in the confidence and power of God while speaking the truth in boldness.

Do you want to see the hearts of people penetrated with the truth of God, rather than their minds? Well speak the weightiness of God in your message and not the wordiness of man. In doing so men will be stripped of their pride and arguments, allowing the word of God to pierce their hearts. Even Paul is a wonderful example of this, because he did not weigh anything on his wording, but everything on the Spirit flowing through his mouth.

For Christ did not send me to baptize but to preach the gospel, and not with words of eloquent wisdom, lest the cross of Christ be emptied of its power. For the word of the cross is folly to those who are perishing, but to us who are being saved it is the power of God. For it is written, "I will destroy the wisdom of the wise, and the discernment of the discerning I will thwart." Where is the one who is wise? Where is the scribe? Where is the debater of this age? Has not God made foolish the wisdom of the world?

1 Corinthians 1:17-20

And I, brethren, when I came to you, came not with excellency of speech or of wisdom, declaring unto you the testimony of God.

For I determined not to know anything among you, save Jesus Christ, and him crucified. And I was with you in weakness, and in fear, and in much trembling. And my speech and my preaching was not with enticing words of man's wisdom, but in demonstration of the Spirit and of power: That your faith should not stand in the wisdom of men, but in the power of God.

1 Corinthians 2:1-5 (KJV)

Paul clearly knew where the power came from in his ministry. The power does not come from his speech or trained mind, it only comes from the Holy Spirit. Now I am not saying that you need to speak in ignorance, or act dumb, but I am saying that your words are inferior compared to God's words. This is done so that men's faith is not in your wisdom but in God's wisdom. Paul walked under the authority of the Lord, and carried out his ministry obediently and correctly by the Spirit.

As has been said previously in this book, we as prophets are to be walking in and under the authority of the Lord, especially when we are speaking forth His word. But with debaters and those who desire prominence they will always question where your authority comes. Even when you are speaking nothing but the truth many people will try to argue it, or tempt you to prove the truth you are speaking. How do we deal with such people, who want to trip us up in the words that we speak?

Let's take a look at how Jesus responded to the religious authority of his day, on this matter.

> And the Pharisees and Sadducees came, and to test him they asked him to show them a sign from heaven. He answered them, "When it is evening, you say, 'It will be fair weather, for the sky is red.' And in the morning, 'It will be stormy today, for the sky is red and threatening.' You know how to interpret the appearance of the sky, but you cannot interpret the signs of the times. An evil and adulterous generation seeks for a sign, but no sign will be given to it except the sign of Jonah." So he left them and departed.
>
> *Matthew 16:1-4*

> And when he entered the temple, the chief priests and the elders of the people came up to him as he was teaching, and said, "By what authority are you doing these things, and who gave you this authority?" Jesus answered them, "I also will ask you one question, and if you tell me the answer,

then I also will tell you by what authority I do these things. The baptism of John, from where did it come? From heaven or from man?" And they discussed it among themselves, saying, "If we say, 'From heaven,' he will say to us, 'Why then did you not believe him?' But if we say, 'From man,' we are afraid of the crowd, for they all hold that John was a prophet." So they answered Jesus, "We do not know." And he said to them, "Neither will I tell you by what authority I do these things.

Matthew 21:23-27

Because of the mighty miracles Jesus did, and because of the Power in the words he was speaking, and because of the Anointing the Father had given him, he had no need to defend himself to hypocrites and scoffers. Yet, in the first account he was tempted to "Prove" himself, and in the second his authority was put into question. But Jesus did not give into such questions and traps for his words. Rather he spoke the truth in the first account and departed, sending the scoffers away. In the latter account he kept his silence by telling them he would give them no answer for their questions.

If we look really close to the ministry of Jesus, we will see why his example proves to us, that debating, quarreling, and strife, are out of the question for those who follow him. First let's look at what Isaiah prophesied about the ministry of Jesus.

This was to fulfill what was spoken by the prophet Isaiah:

Behold, my servant whom I have chosen, my beloved with whom my soul is well pleased. I will put my Spirit upon him, and he will proclaim justice to the Gentiles. He will not quarrel or cry aloud, nor will anyone hear his voice in the streets; a bruised reed he will not break, and a smoldering

wick he will not quench, until he brings justice to victory;
and in his name the Gentiles will hope.

Matthew 12:17–21

Jesus demonstrated to us in his reactions to both the Pharisees and his disciples that he would not debate, quarrel, or strive for a superior position. His whole ministry was to show the disciples and inevitably us, that we serve people by our lives, and not reign over them. This is why he rebuked the disciples in the following passage.

Then the mother of the sons of Zebedee came up to him with her sons, and kneeling before him she asked him for something. And he said to her, "What do you want?" She said to him, "Say that these two sons of mine are to sit, one at your right hand and one at your left, in your kingdom." Jesus answered, "You do not know what you are asking. Are you able to drink the cup that I am to drink?" They said to him, "We are able." He said to them, "You will drink my cup, but to sit at my right hand and at my left is not mine to grant, but it is for those for whom it has been prepared by my Father." And when the ten heard it, they were indignant at the two brothers. But Jesus called them to him and said, "You know that the rulers of the Gentiles lord it over them, and their great ones exercise authority over them. It shall not be so among you. But whoever would be great among you must be your servant, and whoever would be first among you must be your slave, even as the Son of Man came not to be served but to serve, and to give his life as a ransom for many."

Matthew 20:20-28

Jesus clearly demonstrated the heart behind leadership is servanthood. The disciple's mother revealed their heart for personal preference and in the end superiority. Jesus quickly showed them, that serving was the way to leadership. The whole heart of his ministry was to teach us to walk as a servant, and not reign as a Superior Master.

> *A dispute also arose among them, as to which of them was to be regarded as the greatest. And he said to them, "The kings of the Gentiles exercise lordship over them, and those in authority over them are called benefactors. But not so with you. Rather, let the greatest among you become as the youngest, and the leader as one who serves. For who is the greater, one who reclines at table or one who serves? Is it not the one who reclines at table? But I am among you as the one who serves."*

> *Luke 22:24-27*

Here again Jesus states how to lead, and to lead you must serve. Furthermore we must get it into our heads, that mankind is driven to dominate and try to reign superior over others. Even still I am trying to bring forth the point that Debate's are an attempt to prove your point as superior. Jesus did not come to debate or quarrel, furthermore when the devil tried to set a trap for him in the wilderness, Jesus spoke those 3 words of truth in return, and the devil had nothing more to say. Often the devil will use people to try and wrangle with us, and we must be very aware of this when we approach ministry.

Dear friends, if we are armed with God's truth and authority there is no need for us to prove our point through the means of debate. Our main purpose is to speak what has been given to us, and let God bring the point across. We are to let our "Yes" be yes, and our "No" be no, if we go farther than that, then there is the potential for trouble. If you believe you are going to win the lost back to Christ by beating them in debates or arguments, you are wrong. Your intellect may win the physical battle of the mind, but the real battle must be won in the Spirit. In Matthew 7:29 it states that Jesus taught not as one of the Scribes, but with Authority. The Scribes were the intellectuals of that day, yet their teaching seemed to have no authority on it.

Winning arguments through swift speech will not necessarily cause a person to repent, only the power of God can do this. Preaching the Gospel is not intended to win a debate, it is intended to win a soul. This is why we need to be careful when we enter into a conversation with people. We need to quickly discern whether the person(s) has a Spirit of Debate like the devil, or has a voice to Reason, like Jesus. This is why I personally and gently warn against "Christian Debates". Alleged Christian debates are no more than "Spiritual Dog Fights", and this is not reflective of the character of Christ.

There is a time and a place for a reasonable discussion, but you must know whom it is you are talking with, and what spirit is motivating them to talk. If you go into a discussion trying to win or accomplish your point, you must truly question yourself to see if your personal point aligns with God's actual intentions. If you can rejoice in God's truth reigning Superior, then your heart is in the right place, because the ultimate goal of any discussion is that God's truth is found, not that your thoughts abound. Do you rejoice if your agenda wins, or God's truth? The superiority always belongs to God.

If we are standing on top of a matter in Pride, holding God's word, then we are personally glorying in an area that is not ours to glory in. It is God himself & His word that is of eternal superiority. Let's not forget the wonderful mystery of Christ the Cornerstone, for even though it is at the bottom & foundation of all that we do, it is still superior over all that we say.

CHAPTER TWELVE

The Tools and Weapons
of the Prophet

For the word of God is quick, and powerful, and sharper
than any two edged sword, piercing even to the dividing
asunder of soul and spirit, and of the joints and marrow,
and is a discerner of the thoughts and intents of the heart.

Hebrews 4:12 (KJV)

As prophets of the Lord we are called to battle to build, and rebuild. If you are walking in the right spirit and your tongue is anointed correctly, then you will be given the chance to pick up your sword to use for the Lord's purposes. There are several figurative comparisons that are important to discuss in this chapter about the tools & weapons we use in this ministry. Therefore to start this chapter let's look at the heart of prophetic ministry once again. Let's begin with the story of The Good Samaritan.

Jesus replied, "A man was going down from Jerusalem to Jericho, and he fell among robbers, who stripped him and beat him and departed, leaving him half dead. Now by chance a priest was going down that road, and when he saw him he passed by on the other side. So likewise a Levite, when he came to the place and saw him, passed by on the other side. But a Samaritan, as he journeyed, came to where he was, and when he saw him, he had compassion. He went to him and bound up his wounds, pouring on oil and wine. Then he set him on his own animal and brought him to an inn and took care of him. And the next day he took out two denarii and gave them to the innkeeper, saying, 'Take care of him, and whatever more you spend, I will repay you when I come back.' Which of these three, do you think, proved to be a neighbor to the man who fell among the robbers?" He said, "The one who showed him mercy." And Jesus said to him, "You go, and do likewise."

Luke 10:30-37

The key verse which is necessary to bring out from this passage is the following... "He went to him and bound up his wounds, pouring on oil and wine." All prophetic ministry is founded with this heart theme of God. Just because you can hold a sword does not give you the right to wield it around with your own intentions. This is NOT a slash and burn ministry, this is a repent and return ministry.

Yes, we do use the sword of the Lord (His Word) to pierce darkness, lies, deception, etc...but this is an unseen battle fought not with physical hands. Our swords must be dipped at all times with oil and wine when we use them. This oil and wine provide the healing to many existing wounds. If you use this sword without these items of Redemption, you will make the wound larger, and destroy people. It is never acceptable to wield the sword without it being covered by the grace, mercy, redemption, and restoration of the Lord. You should never, take joy in cutting down people who are walking in darkness. Some have wounds, some make wounds, but we are to heal wounds without causing more. So again the heart of prophetic ministry is to speak the truth in love using the sword of the Lord covered, and motivated by the heart of redemption.

If you see the sword of the Lord in a physical manner you will act as Peter did when he cut off the soldier's ear. This story has been addressed already in another chapter, but I wish to remind you again, that you cannot take things into the natural means of warfare. Peter thought it was correct to fight for the Lord's cause by stepping up to defend him in the physical. The reality was, as we all know a soldier lost his ear in the process. But Jesus, seeking to redeem that bad situation, rebuked Peter and healed the soldier's ear in front of everyone. The reality is that we fight an unseen battle in the heavenlies.

> *For we do not wrestle against flesh and blood, but against the rulers, against the authorities, against the cosmic powers over this present darkness, against the spiritual forces of evil in the heavenly places.*

> *Ephesians 6:12*

To better understand this unseen battle we fight, we must look at a few different examples in the Old Testament. The types and symbols of the Old Covenant reveal clearly to us in the New Covenant our approach to ministry. Prophetic ministry is a building and fighting ministry and one of the best examples of this is Nehemiah.

In this story of Nehemiah the children of the Lord are basically still in captivity, though many are starting to be released to head back to Jerusalem. Nehemiah was the cupbearer for the King, and was given permission to return also to help rebuild the wall of the city. Remember the wall of the city had been down for many years in desolation.

The pagans and gentiles were everywhere and had taken over the city.

Yet, God called Nehemiah with a solemn task, "Rebuild the Wall". Not long after he started the project his first wave of ridicule and persecution came.

> *Then I said to them, "You see the trouble we are in, how Jerusalem lies in ruins with its gates burned. Come, let us build the wall of Jerusalem, that we may no longer suffer derision." And I told them of the hand of my God that had been upon me for good, and also of the words that the king had spoken to me. And they said, "Let us rise up and build." So they strengthened their hands for the good work. But when Sanballat the Horonite and Tobiah the Ammonite servant and Geshem the Arab heard of it, they jeered at us and despised us and said, "What is this thing that you are doing? Are you rebelling against the king?" Then I replied to them, "The God of heaven will make us prosper, and we his servants will arise and build, but you have no portion or right or claim in Jerusalem.*
>
> *Nehemiah 2:17-20*

The first wave of attack that came from Sanballat and friends, took the form of sarcastic, and slanderous words, but it wasn't long before their threats took more of a harmful approach. To understand this better we must look at the entirety of Chapter 4 to grasp it best.

> *Now when Sanballat heard that we were building the wall, he was angry and greatly enraged, and he jeered at the Jews. And he said in the presence of his brothers and of the army of Samaria, "What are these feeble Jews doing? Will they restore it for themselves? Will they sacrifice? Will they finish up in a day? Will they revive the stones out of the heaps*

of rubbish, and burned ones at that?" Tobiah the Ammonite was beside him, and he said, "Yes, what they are building— if a fox goes up on it he will break down their stone wall!" Hear, O our God, for we are despised. Turn back their taunt on their own heads and give them up to be plundered in a land where they are captives. Do not cover their guilt, and let not their sin be blotted out from your sight, for they have provoked you to anger in the presence of the builders. So we built the wall. And all the wall was joined together to half its height, for the people had a mind to work. But when Sanballat and Tobiah and the Arabs and the Ammonites and the Ashdodites heard that the repairing of the walls of Jerusalem was going forward and that the breaches were beginning to be closed, they were very angry. And they all plotted together to come and fight against Jerusalem and to cause confusion in it. And we prayed to our God and set a guard as a protection against them day and night. In Judah it was said, "The strength of those who bear the burdens is failing. There is too much rubble. By ourselves we will not be able to rebuild the wall." And our enemies said, "They will not know or see till we come among them and kill them and stop the work." At that time the Jews who lived near them came from all directions and said to us ten times, "You must return to us." So in the lowest parts of the space behind the wall, in open places, I stationed the people by their clans, with their swords, their spears, and their bows. And I looked and arose and said to the nobles and to the officials and to the rest of the people, "Do not be afraid of them. Remember the Lord, who is great and awesome, and fight for your brothers, your sons, your daughters, your wives, and your homes." When our enemies heard that it was known to us and that God had frustrated their plan, we all returned to the wall, each to his work. From that day on, half of my servants worked on construction, and half held the spears, shields, bows, and coats of mail. And the leaders stood behind the whole house of Judah, who were building on the wall. Those who carried burdens were loaded in such a way that each labored on the work with one hand and held his weapon with the other. And each of the builders had his sword strapped at his side while he built. The man who sounded the trumpet was beside me. And I said to the nobles and to the officials and to the rest of the people, "The work is great and widely spread, and we are separated on the wall, far from one another. In the place where you hear the sound of the trumpet, rally to us there. Our God will fight for us." So we labored at the work, and half of them held the spears from the break of dawn until the stars came out. I also said to the people at that time, "Let every man and his servant pass the night within Jerusalem, that they may be a guard for us by night and may labor by day." So neither I nor my brothers nor my servants nor the men of the guard who followed me, none of us took off our clothes; each kept his weapon at his right hand.

Nehemiah Chapter 4

There are several highlights from chapter 4 that reveal many valuable insights we can readily apply to New Covenant ministry. The reality is that the modern church today is in many ways broken and in ruins like the wall of Jerusalem. As prophetic people we come into a situation and see the problems all around. We see the holes and weak spots, and feel very compelled to fix them. It is during these times when the scoffers come to ridicule the work of God. We don't see the walls down as a sad fate of destruction, we see the potential for how they may be rebuilt. So when you put your hands to work, people try to attack you and question why you are bringing attention to weakness. In reality they are calling you a rebel and asking you to turn a blind eye away from the problem.

As stated in previous chapters we are to "Edify" the body of Christ. This simply means to "Build Up". The question then comes, is something broken? The reality is Yes. The devil, false teachers, and false prophets have come in and wreaked havoc on the body of Christ. Furthermore, many Christians themselves have gone the way of the world, and have let the wall come down around them. The Lord Jesus started building his Church through Peter, the disciples and other early church fathers, so we are continuing this work also. Between building and rebuilding there is lots of work to be done in the Body of Christ. Just because you pick up a brick to patch a hole, doesn't mean, you are an accusatory person. It is what prophetic people do, they see a problem, and proceed to fix it. The blessing comes when people recognize the truth in what they say, and join them in the process of rebuilding.

This is why the verse in chapter 4 says: "So we built the wall. And all the wall was joined together to half its height, for the people had a mind to work." If you are confirmed in your message by those around you, this is a blessing while you do the work of rebuilding. However there are plenty of times that your words are not appreciated and you will deal with Sanballats in the process. So when Sanballat and his pack of scoffers came to deeply persecute the work of the Lord, we see how Nehemiah responded correctly.

From that day on, half of my servants worked on construction, and half held the spears, shields, bows, and coats of mail. And the leaders stood behind the whole house of Judah, who were building on the wall. Those who carried burdens were loaded in such a way that each labored on the work with one hand and held his weapon with the other. And each of the builders had his sword strapped at his side while he built. The man who sounded the trumpet was beside me.

Nehemiah 4:16–18

When faced with enemy opposition, the workers could have easily turned away from what they were doing because of peer pressure and fear leaving the wall open, exposed, and unfinished. Rather they joined in the unity of the Spirit and locked arms to both work, and defend the purposes of the Lord. In this story the sword was a physical demonstration of standing for truth. At any moment they would fight to protect the building and restoration project. All walked together in the same mind for the rebuilding of the wall. They used their swords correctly.

Knowing the battle that lies ahead of us, we must be willing to use the "Sword of Truth" while we are in the process of restoring the church the way God intended for it to function. If we don't carry the sword while we work, scoffers, and all false teachers will come in, make camp, and sit upon a wall that is not theirs. We must use the Sword of the Lord like it is mentioned in the following passage:

> *All Scripture is breathed out by God and profitable for teaching, for reproof, for correction, and for training in righteousness, that the man of God may be complete, equipped for every good work.*
>
> *2 Timothy 3:16-17*

We are all like Nehemiah's in our walk today. We have been set free from captivity, and have come into a church whose walls are down, and in need of repair. When you start prophetically speaking to matters in these areas, you better have your sword sharpened and in hand spiritually.

There are some seasons where God uses the Sword in different ways. Sometimes we are not publically speaking to matters, and we must pray prophetic prayers. Even still there are other times when we may not have permission or platform to speak and we must use other means. The word will still go forward, and we must not stop it. An awesome example of using different forms of prophecy is by taking a look at Ezekiel's ministry.

> *The word of the LORD came to me: "Son of man, behold,*

I am about to take the delight of your eyes away from you at a stroke; yet you shall not mourn or weep, nor shall your tears run down. Sigh, but not aloud; make no mourning for the dead. Bind on your turban, and put your shoes on your feet; do not cover your lips, nor eat the bread of men." So I spoke to the people in the morning, and at evening my wife died. And on the next morning I did as I was commanded. And the people said to me, "Will you not tell us what these things mean for us, that you are acting thus?" Then I said to them, "The word of the LORD came to me: 'Say to the house of Israel, Thus says the Lord GOD: Behold, I will profane my sanctuary, the pride of your power, the delight of your eyes, and the yearning of your soul, and your sons and your daughters whom you left behind shall fall by the sword. And you shall do as I have done; you shall not cover your lips, nor eat the bread of men. Your turbans shall be on your heads and your shoes on your feet; you shall not mourn or weep, but you shall rot away in your iniquities and groan to one another. Thus shall Ezekiel be to you a sign; according to all that he has done you shall do. When this comes, then you will know that I am the Lord GOD.' As for you, son of man, surely on the day when I take from them their stronghold, their joy and glory, the delight of their eyes and their soul's desire, and also their sons and daughters, on that day a fugitive will come to you to report to you the news. On that day your mouth will be opened to the fugitive, and you shall speak and be no longer mute. So you will be a sign to them, and they will know that I am the LORD.

Ezekiel 24:15-27

Then we see several chapters later the fulfillment of this prophecy from the Lord.

> *In the twelfth year of our exile, in the tenth month, on*
> *the fifth day of the month, a fugitive from Jerusalem came*
> *to me and said, "The city has been struck down." Now the*
> *hand of the LORD had been upon me the evening before the*
> *fugitive came; and he had opened my mouth by the time the*
> *man came to me in the morning, so my mouth was opened,*
> *and I was no longer mute.*

Ezekiel 33:21-22

If you read commentators or research this section of scripture more, you will find out that this time period of silence was about 3 years. This is really amazing when you think about it. This means that everything between chapters 24 and 33 was not spoken from Ezekiel's mouth, but from his pen. The Lord used these very tough, and sad years to still bring forth his message. The Sword of The Lord, became the Pen of the Lord in Ezekiel's life. This verse from Psalms can clearly portray this theme.

> *To the chief Musician upon Shoshannim, for the sons of*
> *Korah, Maschil, A Song of loves. My heart is inditing a good*
> *matter: I speak of the things which I have made touching*
> *the king: my tongue is the pen of a ready writer.*

Psalms 45:1 (KJV)

We have been put into many different seasons in our lives. Some of which we have the chance to speak to matters verbally, and others like with Ezekiel we have had our mouths closed and had to write instead. This does not mean you are not speaking forth the word of the Lord. Because you are clearly still doing so. Realizing the power of the Word of God, you can prophesy by any means.

Do not despise the "Silent Years", that may come to you, because God is at work in your life regardless of whether your mouth is moving or not. If we do not think God can use Silent Years, then we will not be content in the "Lot" that God gives us (Eccl. 5:19 ESV). Some years there will be speaking, and others there will be writing. Even still there will also be others in praying. All of the above are the Mighty Hand of God at work.

If you despise these quiet years, perhaps you might miss the purpose of the Lord. It is said by Edward Bulwer-Lytton in history that, "The Pen is mightier than the sword!" But rather it should say, the pen is as Mighty as the Sword. If Ezekiel would have given up on the call of the Lord on his life after his wife died and he became mute, he would have never prophesied against the King of Tyre, otherwise known as Lucifer. Read Ezekiel 28, and you will see the words that come against the fallen angel Lucifer. Therefore, make no mistake you can prophesy MIGHTY words of the Lord even if your mouth doesn't open. Darkness cannot remain when the Word of the Lord goes forth in any form. There are however plenty of seasons where we are called to speak to and address matters of concern in the body of Christ. Let me give a good illustration about speaking to matters correctly.

Working as a medical assistant nurse for a few years I had the opportunity to see many amazing scenarios. I love working with people who are sick, and need the help of a doctor. Most of my time as a medical assistant, I spent time in "Urgent Care" situations, though there were some more mild seasons of work in a family practice with minor issues. One of the things that stood out to me in Family Practice work is the skin cancer issues that are rampant among many Americans. People spend way too much time in the sun overexposed to its harmful light, and their skin suffers greatly. So many family doctors' office's set up skin clinics where they remove skin lesions and cancers before they get too bad. I saw many patients come to the clinic and get 3 or 4 different skin issues cut off of their body. (On a side note, stay protected in the sun!!!). The only way to stop skin cancer from spreading is to cut it out entirely. So many, and I do mean many, skin cancers and blemishes were removed from the bodies of patients, and they were sent happily on their way. So the biggest important realization is this, skin cancer can only be stopped by cutting it out. There is no other successful way to remove it. If someone came in with skin cancer, and the Doctor put some ointment on it, and then put a band aid on it, it would not solve the problem what so ever. The skin cancer will only spread if not removed completely from the body. So it is in the Christian body, how we need to realize that there are issues in people's lives that must be dealt with exactly and correctly with a Spiritual Knife. If you do not address the problem, and remove it out of their life, it will only spread and lead inevitably to death, just like with skin cancer. People must see prophetic ministry like that of skin cancer removal. It is not a ministry of mean accusations, but of loving someone enough to tell them the truth and help remove the sin issue in their life.

In this story we can see the value of speaking to a problem, and dealing with it. This scenario involved a cutting, with a sharp instrument. I am comparing this instrument to the Sword of the Lord. In some of the Old Testament accounts we saw that a Sword was used to protect the ministry/work at hand. While in this story we see that the Sword is also used as a precise tool prepped for surgery, not a jagged blade designed for destruction. Not only is the Sword used to defend, it is also used to deliver. In this illustration the problem had to be opened up, and cut out. The effected persons were delivered from their dangerous situations, and lovingly put back to normal. It is in this perfect ministry that once again we can be reminded of the good heart of the Samaritan.

It is one thing to come upon a person bleeding and dying on the side of the road, and we leap to help them. It is quite another to come upon a person with a hidden skin cancer, and have to expose that problem to them. If the wound is open it is easy to pour in oil and wine to restore it. If the wound is closed and not visible, there is often a resistance for removal. Most people don't want you to walk up to them and point out a "Skin Cancer" in their life. They don't acknowledge that there is "sickness" in their body. The reality is, they need to be cut with the Word of the Lord straight to the issue. Truth sometimes hurts, bottom line. This is why when we speak truth to people, we must have a sharp and ready sword, so that the incision is performed correctly to the right size. If you are not using the Word of God correctly, and speak with many doctrinal, and philosophical errors your sword is jagged, and could rip someone where it is not necessary. I am not saying that you must have all of scripture memorized, but rather use it correctly and wisely for the purpose of Redemption.

Let's say for a real example of this that you have a friend who is extremely sarcastic all the time to people. This friend loves the Lord, desires sanctification, hates sin, and lives a moral life, but is a baby Christian. It would be highly wrong to blast this person with 500 scriptures on the fleshly nature, and the road to Hell. In reality, all this Christian needs is one small verse speaking of guarding your tongue. If you hit this person over the head with 500 scriptures and the grips of Hell, you will have used a "Jagged Sword" to swing at them. If you walk in the Spirit in meekness, and tenderness speaking the gentle verse the Lord gave you, then you will have used a sharp sword to deal with the small problem. If someone needs a small skin cancer removed, then don't presume to give them an entire facial reconstruction.

If you are walking with the Lord in the power of the Spirit you will know how to use your sword. There are so many "Christians" even ones who call themselves prophetic, who use a Jagged Sword, and massacre people without love. This jagged sword comes from people who don't know God, his Word, or his loving mercy for everyone. They see the sword as a weapon to destroy instead of a tool to rebuild. Our ministry is wielding a sword, covered in oil and wine. The oil and wine are used for healing; this easily is compared to Redemption and Restoration. We use the sword, and cut deep to the heart of a matter, and when that sword exposes the infection, the oil and wine pour in to heal it immediately upon impact.

Jesus was one of our first examples of using the sword correctly when he spoke Scripture back to the Devil causing him to flee. This is where much of our battling will take place in Prophetic ministry. Knowing the scriptures allows you to thrust your sword back at the devil to send him fleeing. Whereas with "Growing Christians" your sword will be used more gently to pull a bad tooth, cut out a skin cancer, or open a cyst to let an infection drain out and heal. We fight aggressively with our sword against the devil, but when it comes to fellow brothers and sisters we put our gentle Surgeon's hands on, and cautiously perform Spiritual surgery for the Lord.

Even though this chapter is spoken largely in a figurative way, there is still that reality of war. When the walls are down, weeds have grown, and sheep have infections, we must know how to handle the Tools and Weapons that the Lord gives us properly. Sometimes we have to come in and hack a bunch of weeds out of a place brought in by years of lethargy or laziness. Sometimes we have to come into a situation and help rebuild the wall broken down by the enemy. Sometimes the sheep are sick and in need of a doctor. But if you walk in on "your mission" instead of God's mission you could do far greater damage. The sword God gives us is for His purposes not ours. But we must not be afraid to pick it up and learn how to use it. If your sword is jagged from bitterness, or much fighting, then get alone with God and let him sharpen it with his word. If you can't hold up your sword because your arms are not strong enough, then spend time with him in His word, and he will cause you to rise up on Eagle's wings. He has given you a tool that can also be a weapon, do you know which one he wants you to use today?

> And take the helmet of salvation, and the sword of the Spirit, which is the word of God
>
> *Ephesians 6:17*

> By the word of truth, by the power of God, by the armour of righteousness on the right hand and on the left...
>
> *2 Corinthians 6:7 (KJV)*

> Doctors are not allowed to start performing surgery until they have passed their classes, and soldiers are not allowed to fight until they have completed training. Even so prophets must complete both of these, or you will not be allowed to use the Tools and Weapons of the Lord.

Section 3

Dangers to The Prophetic Calling

CHAPTER THIRTEEN

The Lies of the Devil and Society

Let's now move into our next section, which discusses some of the dangers prophetic ministry encounters. Even though this is not a large section, and the chapters may be smaller, their content is none-the-less important. This first chapter reveals the origins and intentions of the devil against the word of God, and all who are called to live by and speak it. This chapter is not about avoiding society, but recognizing how much the devil has influenced society, and how much society has influenced the church. This chapter exposes how society has in many ways "set up camp" in our territory, and is attempting to thwart the work of God.

The entire agenda of the devil through society is to lie to you, and tell you there is No Wall At All for you to fight on. Yet God has called many of us to walk in a prophetic calling, and we do have a position to stand in, on the wall. The devil, and society wish to prevent you from serving the Lord. So the devil puts on the cloaks of society to disengage you from the war. We are part of the City of God, and there is a wall for us to stand on, but the devil would like us to believe otherwise. This is why he has been lying to us from the beginning.

The First Lie: "Hath God Said?" The very first words recorded in scripture from the devil's mouth are...

> *Now the serpent was more subtle than any beast of the field which the LORD God had made. And he said unto the woman, Yea, hath God said, Ye shall not eat of every tree of the garden?*
>
> *Genesis 3:1 (KJV)*

In the beginning, God created everything with His word, and all things were good. And in that same beginning the devil was already at work trying to twist and pervert God's pure Word. God did say not to eat, but the devil raised the first "Doubtful Question" and took man's heart away from truth in God's word. The devil was already working to manipulate man, by questioning God's character and word. This is the foundation for all "form criticism" that we experience in our society. Man should have known better than to believe a lie from the devil. For even Jesus said...

> *He was a murderer from the beginning, and does not stand in the truth, because there is no truth in him. When he lies, he speaks out of his own character, for he is a liar and the father of lies.*
>
> *John 8:44b*

It is from this foundation that we see the entire flawed character of the devil come forth towards man, as well as God's word. It is this same character that fuels everything in our current modern evil society. If you take a look at each of the common channels of thinking today, each one's foundation is that of "Questioning Truth", mainly Biblical Truth. God is Truth, and all that he has said, he will do, and the devil cannot boast of this in his own character.

The main channels of modern thinking include; humanism, universalism, individualism, materialism, psychology, co-existing, moral relativism, and the list goes on. It is very important to briefly define these few terms so that you can get a better sense of how they may look when they come your way. Once again these channels of modern thought have deluged the body of Christ, and we must uproot these pagan, and demonic forms of thought. All of their origins are from the devil, and none can be trusted.

Many of these terms can be found by searching the internet on various dictionary sites. They may vary from site to site in wording, and depending on the site will have differing levels of theology foundations or secular origins. The ones I have picked capture best the ideas I am trying to illustrate in this chapter.

Humanism: "A doctrine or way of life centered on human interests or values, devotion to the humanities."

Humanist: "One versed in the knowledge of human nature."

Universalism: "In theology, the doctrine or belief that all men will be saved or made happy in a future life."

Unitarian: "One who denies the doctrine of the trinity, and ascribes divinity to God the Father only. A member of a religious denomination stressing individual freedom or belief."

Unitarianism: "The doctrines of Unitarians, who contend for the unity of the Godhead, in opposition to the Trinitarians, and who of course deny the divinity of Christ."

Materialism: "The doctrine of materialists; the opinion of those who maintain that the soul of man is not a spiritual substance distinct from matter, but that it is the result or effect or the organization of matter in the body. A preoccupation with material rather than spiritual things."

Co-Exist: "To exist together or at the same time, to live in peace with each other."

Individualism: "A doctrine that the interests of the individual are primary."

Individualist: "One that pursues a markedly independent course in thought or action."

Hedonism: "The doctrine that pleasure is the chief good in life."

Narcissism: "Un-due dwelling on one's own self or attainments, someone who falls in love with their own image."

Moral Relativism: "Subjective reasoning that determines what is right or wrong in one's own eyes. All aspects of truth molds to one's own personal constitution. Whatever seems right for each person in each situation, as determined by each one's choices."

Psychology: "A discourse or treatise on the human soul; or the doctrine of the nature and properties of the soul. The science of mind and behavior."

Tolerance: "Sympathy or indulgence for beliefs or practices differing from one's own. The allowable deviation from a standard."

Politically Correct: "Conforming to a belief that language and practices which could offend sensibilities should be eliminated."

Our entire society's belief system can be summed up in the above definitions. Yet, the joint theme of them all is Anti-God. All of these definitions complement and "pat" one another on the back except when it is a Christian's back. If you are like me, I for sure rise up in holy unction and fire when I read these terms. They are utterly demonic, and have taken over our society with intense force. This is why the world hates God, Jesus, the Holy Spirit, and all Christians, because the word of God is ALL TRUTH. All of these other forms of thinking, deny any real truth and turn all words into subjective "patty cake".

It's one thing to relate with lost people who believe these forms of philosophy, but it is a totally different thing to try and relate with those who think this way and call themselves believers. This is why this type of thinking is so dangerous, and destructive to the Christian walk. These philosophies have crept in by massive amounts into the modern church. You have some churches sounding more like "Unitarians" than Christians. Churches take out the message of the Cross, because it is too offensive. Other churches take out holiness, because it goes against their own "Selfish" desires and moral beliefs. People are being counseled in churches today with "Man's Psychology" and put on drugs for problems that only God can heal through Jesus. Truly we live in a society that is "Self Centered, Self Absorbed, and Self Governed". A place where man's so called wisdom tries to trump God's Absolute wisdom.

In so many ways the messages coming across the platforms are an easy "beliefism", with no accountability for sin, and no message of repentance preached. "Political Correctness" has watered down the Gospel, and individualism, has watered down the heart of God, which is to have a corporate body. Christ wants a body, but the world wants an individual. Such a belief separates God's people from truth, and from being connected to each other. Hedonism, plagues many Christians with worthless living, to no avail. While narcissism, has taken captive many Christians into self love and expression. People now have itchy ears, and appetites for fluff sermons and opinions. There are even other massive problems with tolerance and co-existence in the church. Sin is not preached about or dealt with, leaving the church body in darkness, with open wounds. This topic could go on and on, and on about how the lies and agenda of the devil have crept into the church, but the best place to confirm this is by scripture.

> *Preach the word; be instant in season, out of season; reprove, rebuke, exhort with all longsuffering and doctrine. For the time will come when they will not endure sound doctrine; but after their own lusts shall they heap to themselves teachers, having itching ears; And they shall turn away their ears from the truth, and shall be turned unto fables.*
>
> *2 Timothy 4:2-4 (KJV)*

> But understand this, that in the last days there will come times of difficulty. For people will be lovers of self, lovers of money, proud, arrogant, abusive, disobedient to their parents, ungrateful, unholy, heartless, unappeasable, slanderous, without self-control, brutal, not loving good, treacherous, reckless, swollen with conceit, lovers of pleasure rather than lovers of God, having the appearance of godliness, but denying its power. Avoid such people.
>
> *2 Timothy 3:1-5*

The problem comes in avoiding such people! When you live and interact with many who walk this way, sometimes your whole church is filled with "Worldly Christians, or Carnal Christians". These stay in sin, because the truth of the Gospel is not preached. Anyone who preaches so called "biblical messages" without full exposition of scripture needs to be noted in your mind. Here are two amazing quotes from Matthew Henry about all of these topics...

(In regards to bad teachers...) "Those are the most dangerous seducers who suggest to sinners that which tends to lessen their dread of sin, and their fear of God. (Furthermore...) "It is ill with those people who can better hear pleasing lies, than unpleasing truths."

The entire demonic agenda is for God's word to be overturned by questions, arguments, offenses, accusations, at the core both loveless and based on lawlessness. The devil's entire goal is to cause any "Light" for the Lord to turn off and not burn. The devil wants to smooth over the hard truths of the Bible. He also wants your bright beacon of truth to be put under a bushel. His whole agenda is to turn off your light, and create compromise on your part. Therefore the entire outcome of the philosophy of society and the devil is to create, "MOOD LIGHTING". If the devil can't get you to turn off your light, his next attempt will be to get you to turn it down, or put a shade on it.

Here is a small illustration about mood lighting that will paint a better picture for this topic. In the latter years many of us have grown to hate florescent lights because of how unnatural and strong they are for the eyes. So instead of using the overhead florescent lights we have adapted smaller light fixtures in the corners with soft bulb wattage. This is the perfect essence of mood lighting in a decorative atmosphere. Unfortunately this is the same thing that is happening in the body of Christ. People who are called to be "Lighthouses" for the Lord with his Blazing Light of Truth, are now toning down their words, which quench their light and diminish their impact, moving them to be a table lamp instead of a Harbor Beacon. Is this not so? One of the ways that this happens is because "Christians" including prophetic people, have bought into the lies of the world, and they have compromised ceasing to speak and exhort truthfully. People love darkness and they do not want real light to be in their midst. This is why they will hate you for speaking the truth in your ministry.

Here again is what the Bible says about this.

And this is the judgment: the light has come into the world, and people loved the darkness rather than the light because their works were evil. For everyone who does wicked things hates the light and does not come to the light, lest his works should be exposed. But whoever does what is true comes to the light, so that it may be clearly seen that his works have been carried out in God.

John 3:19-21

In the natural process away from Truth you will eventually end up in total darkness. God is light, and so is His Truth, anything away from that is darkness. If you walk away from truth, you will eventually compromise and put a shade over your "smaller" light, and then finally you will blend in with the darkness and become numb to any exhortations whatsoever. This is why many Christians cannot handle true prophetic ministry. They say, "Stop speaking to this matter, stop shining a light on this, Come on you are too bright, stop exposing this sin.!" When people stop exhorting one another daily about sin or carnality, they become dull and numb to its consequences.

Take care, brothers, lest there be in any of you an evil, unbelieving heart, leading you to fall away from the living God. But exhort one another every day, as long as it is called "today," that none of you may be hardened by the deceitfulness of sin.

Hebrews 3:12-13

Once your light is out, then the grips of sin catch up with you, and you conform into the ways of the rest who wandered off the path of truth, following something contrary to God's Word.

Now the Spirit speaketh expressly, that in the latter times some shall depart from the faith, giving heed to seducing spirits, and doctrines of devils; Speaking lies in hypocrisy; having their conscience seared with a hot iron...

1 Timothy 4:1-2 (KJV)

This is the cold, hard reality of the devil's first lie. "Hath God Said?" When we start to question God, his Truth, or anything about Him, we then become prone to the doctrines of the devil. The word of God is 100% true, and God is 100% real, if you believe anything otherwise you will not walk in correct prophetic ministry.

When you believe the devil and the lies of society your mind will become scarred and numb. For this next section I would like to include a full illustration from an earlier book I wrote in a series called *Exhortations from a Clay Pot.*

Scarred & Numb Minds (Taken from Book 1 of the series).

More Christians walk around with scars than ever before in this day and age. These scars are not from battle wounds, or from warfare. These scars are not even visible to the naked eye. These scars are on the mind, and they come from bad daily habits established in our lives. Too often our fellow Christians in these last days have rationalized integrating themselves into worldly pursuits through daily habits. For example, how much of your personal time is spent watching movies and television? How many movies or television shows have you watched in this week? How many hours have you spent watching frivolous nothings that are pre-recorded, and marked for your special viewing later? Compare this preoccupation with how much time you spend in Bible study and communion with the Lord.

There is an utter obsession for media in this society that has skyrocketed out of control in the past 30 years. Never have I seen such an enemy's hand so visible as how God, family and the roles of men and women are clearly undermined in both movies and television series programming. The voice of the enemy is stronger than ever before in our homes and businesses. Horror films cover the shelves of rental stores, and these movies flock the theaters every dark holiday. What is more detestable, are the number of Christians in attendance! I am utterly shocked by what I hear in the form of rationalization that comes from the mouths of "believers".

These Christians say that they know the difference between Good and Evil, and are not bothered by it. Well I know the difference between a poisonous snake and a non-poisonous one, but it doesn't mean I should go and pick it up to play with. Many believers do not demonstrate wise discernment and it is because sound judgment is produced through practice as our senses are trained to discern good and evil. Hebrews 5:14 tells us that the "powers of discernment are trained by constant practice to distinguish good from evil." When we wallow in the muck, our insight is dulled.

I have even heard of fellow Christians smoking on a normal basis, and attending bars on a regular basis. Seriously this is not a matter to be taken lightly. Christians have totally bought into the lies of the enemy, and blend in well with today's culture. Where are the Lights for the Lord shining amidst all of this. I can no longer distinguish Christians anymore; they are often times immersed into this present world. Their conscience's are scarred and numbed because of the filthy input from the world.

Their eyes bring in sexuality, violence, immorality, and filth. Their ears bring in the vulgarity, rebellion, abominations, and slanderous themes. Their mouths bring in smoke, excessive strong drink, and gluttony into their bodies.

With true compassionate intense love I say, "Please STOP AND THINK!" Do you not know that you are the temple of the Living God who dwells inside of you. Have you not heard that there should be no other gods in the presence of our Savior? The things that we are allowing into our bodies and minds are giving the enemy footholds into active parts of our lives. How can our Lord Jesus Christ share and walk on the same path as these detestable movies, shows, and toxins? Can you believe that I have even heard youth pastors say that they watch these movies and programs to relate with the youth audience they preach to. This is the most absurd thing I have ever heard. I say relate to them with Jesus Christ and Him alone. You don't need to use the hands of the devil to reach those students. What you need is confidence in preaching, as Paul said "this one thing I preach, Jesus Christ Crucified."

The problem is, that the minds, consciences and standards of our fellow Christians are failing. Their minds are scarred, and flawed. No longer can they detect the filth coming into the Lord's temple. After all if you have asked Jesus to come into your life, He has come to dwell inside of you, and these things of the world cannot dwell next to God the Holy Ghost.

Jesus deserves a clean mind, clean eyes, clean ears, and clean heart. If we have committed ourselves to the Lord's purposes, we must give Him all areas, and all our habits. Society wants to dull our senses to right and wrong.

Let me continue and tell you an amazing illustration on this topic. For many years growing up I spent time with my good friend Greg who liked some of the same things in life as I did. Greg is a very active person. He lives on the wild side, and is into many outside hobbies. Motorcycles, boating, hiking, music, and working with cars. I would sum him up as a "Life Enthusiast". He lives life to the fullest by no understatement of the word. Then an accident came one day to him and changed many things.

Greg was cooking on the stove at his home, and the pan of grease knocked over onto his arm. Having caught somewhat on fire, the scalding grease burnt his right arm to shreds. He spent many days in a special burn facility, and underwent many surgeries to replace the missing skin. There is no doubt about it, his arm and hand are quite unpleasant to look at. Truly his arm a sight that causes people to look a second time.

There is only a small layer of grafted skin covering his tendons, veins and muscles. This skin layer is almost transparent, and there are no nerves left whatsoever. What is totally interesting about this is the fact that Greg cannot feel anything on this part of his arm. He told me just awhile back that he was working on the engine of a car, and had apparently slipped causing a large cut on his arm. Greg did not notice it, because he did not feel it. Therefore he bled profusely for an hour or so until he saw the blood. This is incredibly alarming for him, because he has to be so careful to pay attention to things like this, or he could very well bleed to death. Greg's burn, truly is a vivid picture of what this passage in Timothy is talking about.

Now the Spirit speaketh expressly, that in the latter times some shall depart from the faith, giving heed to seducing spirits, and doctrines of devils; Speaking lies in hypocrisy; having their conscience seared with a hot iron...

1 Timothy 4:1-2 (KJV)

Paul in this passage is stating that their minds (conscience's) had been seared or burned with a hot iron, preventing them from properly functioning. If you take a hot iron and touch it to your brain, it will totally destroy that section of brain, never to be fixed again by any human hands. The brain is so delicate and any hot iron would totally destroy whatever it would touch. This is why Paul is using such vivid descriptions with these people, because this is what was happening to them.

Today we see this happening everywhere we go. Christians are saying, "It is ok to watch this movie, it will not bother me." Or they will say, "This language and vulgarity doesn't bother me." Or "I am not offended by their actions, or drinking." These same Christians that have rationalized these standards away, are the same ones who consciences have been burnt by the hot iron of this evil world we live in. They say, "Well I am not offended by this language or when people say the Lord's name in vain". In return to that, I say, well you may not be offended, but the Lord God almighty is totally offended with it. Here is something to ponder; if the Lord's name is taken in vain even just once in a movie, it's not something this temple needs to be watching. Is it more sinful to hear the Lord's name in vain once or 20 times? Let's put it this way, all of HEAVEN is shocked if the Lord's name is said in vain.

To close on this topic, I must say with sincerity, please reconsider what your normal acceptable habits are. We are not here to be comfortable and enjoy media, we are here to reach the lost. If movies, television, and other worldly practices are ramped in your life, then you are numb. If language, violence, immorality, and shame upon the Lord Jesus Christ does not bother you, then your conscience has failed. If you do not cringe when sin is committed around you, then you have scarred your mind, and something needs to be done.

If you find yourself like this, then only Jesus can restore your mind to its fine tuned delicate state of awareness. Let us draw close to the Lord for His healing hands to work upon our numb and scarred minds. As our conscience's truly come alive, you will find out that almost everything in society, and that's media driven will set off Red Flags!

Scarred & Numb Minds,   *Exhortations from a Clay Pot Book 1*

After looking at the outcome of lies from the devil and society, we are left asking the question, "How do we stay clear of this dangerous road of deception?" The reality is the lies and agenda of the devil have so infiltrated the world, and believers that it's hard to discern right from wrong. Even when you do discern right from wrong, the effects of society flank any truth from being shared. The whole point they want to accomplish is, "Leave us alone, to sin or live how we desire, it's my life, and I will do what I want." Furthermore many so called Christians who have bought into these lies then become your opposition to speaking truth, and take arms with the devil.

The reality is we have a wall to fight on, and we cannot run away from this battle. If you turn off your light, or put a shade on it, you are in danger of becoming numb to truth. But if you realize what God's purpose is for your life, you will not compromise away truth for the sake of "relating with people better". The answer to winning this battle, and the way to attain it correctly is by having the full Armor of God on, before you go into war. But so many Christians have taken off their armor to be closer to the world. The only way to get close to the world is to withdraw from your place on the wall and to step down to a compromising level of worldliness. We must highly consider the truth of this passage from Ephesians before we walk the prophetic journey, or any aspect of the Christian life.

> *Finally, be strong in the Lord and in the strength of his might. Put on the whole armor of God, that you may be able to stand against the schemes of the devil. For we do not wrestle against flesh and blood, but against the rulers, against the authorities, against the cosmic powers over this*

present darkness, against the spiritual forces of evil in the heavenly places. Therefore take up the whole armor of God, that you may be able to withstand in the evil day, and having done all, to stand firm. Stand therefore, having fastened on the belt of truth, and having put on the breastplate of righteousness, and, as shoes for your feet, having put on the readiness given by the gospel of peace. In all circumstances take up the shield of faith, with which you can extinguish all the flaming darts of the evil one; and take the helmet of salvation, and the sword of the Spirit, which is the word of God, praying at all times in the Spirit, with all prayer and supplication. To that end keep alert with all perseverance, making supplication for all the saints.

Ephesians 6:10-18

The entire war for so many Christians is in the mind, and this is why we must have the Helmet of Salvation. This key component is the victory to winning many of the battles we face. The helmet is the word of God accompanied with the Mind of Christ, and these foundational aspects bring to our mind His truth at all times. If we are not daily in the word, then the mind of Christ will not be as audible to our hearts. Staying in the word, by the power of the Holy Spirit enriches us, equips us, and solidifies us, so that we may be strong and fight in the day of battle. The day of battle is everyday walking in the light while living in a system steeped in darkness. As it has been said earlier, if you walk away from truth you will start to question God. Therefore wearing his truth on your mind, heart and life protects you from the deceitfulness and darts of the enemy.

If you are getting ready to go into battle, I also recommend you deal with your own questions first, and any lies you may have been told by the devil. Because if you put your armor on, over the lies, then there is a large chance you could be attacked from inside your own flesh. You must remove every lie from the devil or society, and replace it with the truth of God's word. Having armor on top of lies is just as dangerous as walking around with no armor at all.

After your armor is on successfully you must always be watchful for the attacks of the devil. His lies will try and detour you from your mission of redemption. The devil will try to question your motives. He will try and tell you not to talk to the sheep. He will also tell the sheep that they are not in need of any doctors. If the sheep stay sick, the devil is accomplishing his goal to steal, kill and destroy.

When the light gets too close then the devil puts on humanism and other cloaks to destroy your credibility and message. They will tell you that your exhortations are accusations. They will suggest to you that your pure convictions are condemnations. These lies will stop you from admonishing and persuade you to tolerate sin. In all of this God's truth is being replaced with a lie.

Others may enjoy mood lighting and feel comfortable with it, but you may not. Others may enjoy watching junk on television, but you should not. You cannot walk in the same manner as the rest of the world, or carnal Christians. There is a war going on, and we must be prepared to stand our ground while the darkness is around. If you compromise the truth of God by believing the lies of society and the devil, you will then become the classic example of a "Political Chaplain". We all know what this is don't we? A political chaplain says the right smooth words out of two sides of their mouth, in whatever situation they may be in. They can be a priest for a Catholic, while in the same day they can be a monk for a Lutheran, or a Minister for a Baptist. Yet even still many "Political Chaplains" are best described as "Religious Chameleons". They change their color to adapt to present circumstances. This type of mentality is deceitful and leads many astray from the path of righteousness. Straying towards humanism leads many to believe that everything is ok, and God will take everyone to heaven regardless how they live. We cannot and will not become Political Chaplains in the true journey of Prophetic Ministry. God and His Word do not change; therefore his message is still the same and does not need to be molded to any humanistic thought. A sin is a sin, it's black or white, because all have sinned and fallen short of the glory of God. When people deny truth, they actually reveal they care nothing about God's plan, and want to indulge their lives how they wish. If we believe anything other than God, as ultimate truth we are in great danger.

God is not man, that he should lie, or a son of man, that he should change his mind. Has he said, and will he not do it? Or has he spoken, and will he not fulfill it?

Numbers 23:19

Indeed, let God be true but every man a liar.

Romans 3:4b (NKJV)

In conclusion for this chapter, anything outside of the word of God, should be questioned entirely. You have a purpose in a ministry of Redemption and Restoration and if the enemy sees you he will do anything he can to stop your ministry of Medical War Relief. We are medics for the Lord prophetically, and we must carry the word of God and use it's medicine on the wounds of people. Because this war is so strong we must wear complete armor even while attempting to be a doctor for wounded soldiers. Do not listen to lies of the devil, but continue to walk in the path God has compelled you to walk in. Wear your armor, live in the Word, and Get on the wall, there are many who need healing, and refreshing. In the face of the devil's opposition do not give into the temptation of shying away from a difficult battle, God will protect and be with you.

You must know and embrace the Truth's of God,

or you cannot face the Lies of the Devil.

CHAPTER FOURTEEN

Watchmen Under Fire

Now that you are in a real battle, let's discuss where the fire comes from. We are under siege from within and beyond our walls. In this chapter let's talk about both sides of the wall. Let's also talk about some ways that you get fired upon, and how to guard yourself in such attacks. You're on a wall and visible to the enemy and to the church, unfortunately bullets can come at you from both directions. The entire reason the enemy uses outside sources and inside sources to shoot at you, is because he does not want the Prophetic Ministry of Redemption and Restoration coming out of your mouth. But with God as your banner of protection you will make it through.

When God places you on the wall to be a seer, it is because he wants you to pray and warn others about the dangers of the coming enemy into the church or against the church. The point of this chapter is not to define all the different "types" of spirits that attack us, rather it is about how we respond to their attacks. Many of the outside bullets that come to you in your ministry are very easy to identify. Let's take a look at a few easy tactics of the enemy. This first example is that of Bar-Jesus.

> *When they had gone through the whole island as far as Paphos, they came upon a certain magician, a Jewish false prophet named Bar-Jesus. He was with the proconsul, Sergius Paulus, a man of intelligence, who summoned Barnabas and Saul and sought to hear the word of God. But Elymas the magician (for that is the meaning of his name) opposed them, seeking to turn the proconsul away from the faith. But Saul, who was also called Paul, filled with the Holy Spirit, looked intently at him and said, "You son of the devil, you enemy of all righteousness, full of all deceit and villainy, will you not stop making crooked the straight paths of the Lord? And now, behold, the hand of the Lord is upon you, and you will be blind and unable to see the sun for a time." Immediately mist and darkness fell upon him, and he went about seeking people to lead him by the hand. Then the proconsul believed, when he saw what had occurred, for he was astonished at the teaching of the Lord.*

> *Acts 13:6-12*

In this situation it was easy to tell that Bar-Jesus was of an enemy spirit. He opposed emphatically the work of God, and tried to hinder the Gospel from reaching the Proconsul. Yet Paul filled with the Spirit knew the attack and dealt with it immediately with the heart of redemption in mind, because when he spoke against Bar-Jesus blindness came from the Lord for only a short season. Knowing God's heart he wanted to redeem that person from the grips of the devil. The Proconsul believed because of the judgment and the Gospel moved forward. Nothing will stop the forward motion of the Gospel of Jesus Christ. For the next example let's again look at another moment in Paul's ministry where another attack came from outside the wall, against the movement of the Gospel.

> *As we were going to the place of prayer, we were met by*
> *a slave girl who had a spirit of divination and brought her*
> *owners much gain by fortune-telling. She followed Paul and*
> *us, crying out, "These men are servants of the Most High*
> *God, who proclaim to you the way of salvation." And this*
> *she kept doing for many days. Paul, having become greatly*
> *annoyed, turned and said to the spirit, "I command you in*
> *the name of Jesus Christ to come out of her." And it came out*
> *that very hour. But when her owners saw that their hope of*
> *gain was gone, they seized Paul and Silas and dragged them*
> *into the marketplace before the rulers. And when they had*
> *brought them to the magistrates, they said, "These men are*
> *Jews, and they are disturbing our city.*

Acts 16:16-20

Again it is clear to see the outward display of enemy attacks from evil spirits in this story. In this scenario a lying spirit took hold of a girl and brought visibility to the ministry of Paul & Silas. They were walking on a wall, and carrying the message of the Gospel forward, and this lying spirit desired to expose them in their place of battle and ministry. This attack came not long after they started to pray. Paul quickly became annoyed and dealt with the evil spirit, while setting the girl free in the process. Her life was spared, but Paul cared not of the income she made for her owners. The owners hated the fact that she was restored and they lost their money from her captivity. Fierce persecution arose, and then Paul and Silas were accused of disturbing the peace of the city's normal way of life. This same reality will happen to any of us, when we overturn the ways of darkness. The world's economy will suffer because of the freeing power of Jesus Christ. However we must not be afraid to set the captives free at any cost.

For the next example let's briefly visit again the ministry of Nehemiah. Nehemiah had received permission from the king to relocate back to Israel and start to rebuild the wall. His whole purpose was to rebuild and repair what was broken down and left in shambles. The enemy had set up camp, and was really cozy, lording themselves over the people. But when the bright light of the Lord came to town, it exposed the dark forces at work. Nehemiah's intentions were to redeem, and restore what was lost.

> *But when Sanballat the Horonite and Tobiah the Ammonite*
> *servant heard this, it displeased them greatly that someone*
> *had come to seek the welfare of the people of Israel.*
>
> *Nehemiah 2:10*

In the prophetic ministry we seek to repair the well-being of hurting and wounded sheep. Many will be opposed to this ministry, because they like their sin and dominion. But Nehemiah filled with the Spirit of the Lord responded in this way...

> *Then I replied to them, "The God of heaven will make*
> *us prosper, and we his servants will arise and build, but you*
> *have no portion or right or claim in Jerusalem.*
>
> *Nehemiah 2:20*

Just like Nehemiah had a word from God to perform his task, so we too, walking in the prophetic calling must know our words from God and stand properly in them. If you see clearly the enemy attack coming, then you must warn the people correctly. It is your place, job, and fulfillment of God's plan to do this.

Now to move on to the next illustration let's talk about one enemy that can attack us both from the outside, and from the inside. This is about the Spirit of Jezebel. Of course we all know the Old Testament account of this evil person, and what she tried to do against Elijah. The power of influence and the tongue of the devil propelled her at rapid rates against the ministry of Elijah. Her attacks came clearly from the outside of the wall at the beginning. So let's look at some of the highlights from that story.

Elijah has just finished the "Baal Prophets Showdown", leaving the

400 prophets dead, and the glory of God revealed to many people. Elijah made a public humiliation of their fraudulent ministry and moved in the mighty power of the Lord. When Ahab heard about this, he then spoke to his wife Jezebel. This is where we will pick up the highlights of the story.

Ahab told Jezebel all that Elijah had done, and how he had killed all the prophets with the sword. Then Jezebel sent a messenger to Elijah, saying,

> *"So may the gods do to me and more also, if I do not make your life as the life of one of them by this time tomorrow." Then he was afraid, and he arose and ran for his life and came to Beersheba, which belongs to Judah, and left his servant there. But he himself went a day's journey into the wilderness and came and sat down under a broom tree. And he asked that he might die, saying, "It is enough; now, O LORD, take away my life, for I am no better than my fathers." And he lay down and slept under a broom tree. And behold, an angel touched him and said to him, "Arise and eat."*
>
> *1 Kings 19:1-5*

It is amazing to see the power of one evil spirit at work against a man of God. Elijah had just seen the mighty hand of God destroy 400 false prophets, who could have easily taken Elijah out. God did not let 400 overcome 1; rather he overcame 400 by his 1. Then the evil Jezebel rose up in anger, and declared war against Elijah. This man of God went into a state of fear, left his wall as a watchman, and fled into the wilderness. Yet the mercy of the Lord met this man of God, restored him with food and drink, and took him into a deeper place of communion in the process. What mercy God had, even when His man, fled from an evil woman.

It is clear through scripture that the Spirit of Jezebel is often at work also in today's church scene. Let's take a look at the New Testament reference to this enemy.

And to the angel of the church in Thyatira write: 'The words of the Son of God, who has eyes like a flame of fire, and whose feet are like burnished bronze. 'I know your works, your love and faith and service and patient endurance, and that your latter works exceed the first. But I have this against you, that you tolerate that woman Jezebel, who calls herself a prophetess and is teaching and seducing my servants to practice sexual immorality and to eat food sacrificed to idols. I gave her time to repent, but she refuses to repent of her sexual immorality. Behold, I will throw her onto a sickbed, and those who commit adultery with her I will throw into great tribulation, unless they repent of her works, and I will strike her children dead. And all the churches will know that I am he who searches mind and heart, and I will give to each of you according to your works.

Revelation 2:18-23

The 4 key words to these verses are; "Seducing" "Prophetess" "Tolerate" "My Servants". The Jezebel spirit takes on so many forms to accomplish her agenda of dominate control and destruction. If anger doesn't work, she forms her words into fine drips of seducing honey. In the case of Elijah she used anger, in the case of the modern church she uses flattery. These aggressive attempts of persuasion are to steer the man of God off the wall and into her arms of control. We must never move to serve one such spirit by tolerating such lawlessness. It has been stated in previous chapters, the true Spirit of God NEVER uses flattery to control people. This is one of Jezebel's greatest and most common weapons.

Beware....of such "leaders of influence" who intend to use sorcery with their words for an outcome of personal influence, in which they flank their words as a prophecy from God, when in reality it is nothing more than natural human speculation, or persuasion. Those who speak the oracles of God CARE NOTHING of human persuasion, but wholly depend on God's communication. The following verses bear this out.

He shall seduce with flattery those who violate the covenant, but the people who know their God shall stand firm and take action.

Daniel 11:32

With her much fair speech she caused him to yield, with the flattering of her lips she forced him. He goeth after her straightway, as an ox goeth to the slaughter, or as a fool to the correction of the stocks; Till a dart strike through his liver; as a bird hasteth to the snare, and knoweth not that it is for his life.

Proverbs 7:21-23 (KJV)

Make no mistake that the Spirit of Jezebel desires to destroy and kill like her father the devil. If she cannot succeed by shooting you off the wall, she will try to woo you off the wall and into her arms, with intentions to kill you.

There are still other spirits that try to attack your position on the wall from the inside, and these are the "religiously deceived" people. The spirit of Religion and Worldliness has come upon many people and they flat out despise hearing truth from God's Prophets.

For they are a rebellious people, lying children, children unwilling to hear the instruction of the LORD; who say to the seers, "Do not see," and to the prophets, "Do not prophesy to us what is right; speak to us smooth things, prophesy illusions, leave the way, turn aside from the path, let us hear no more about the Holy One of Israel.

Isaiah 30:9-11

Continuing there are other "Religiously Deceived" people who portray to you that they like you and the word that you bring forth. However these people too, you must be guarded against, for they are in the wrong spirit.

> *As for you, son of man, your people who talk together about you by the walls and at the doors of the houses, say to one another, each to his brother, 'Come, and hear what the word is that comes from the LORD.' And they come to you as people come, and they sit before you as my people, and they hear what you say but they will not do it; for with lustful talk in their mouths they act; their heart is set on their gain. And behold, you are to them like one who sings lustful songs with a beautiful voice and plays well on an instrument, for they hear what you say, but they will not do it. When this comes—and come it will!—then they will know that a prophet has been among them.*
>
> *Ezekiel 33:30-33*

These people may listen to you for a season, and you may think you are gaining ground with them, but always keep cautious because when the word goes to the bone, and they may turn into venomous serpents and come against you. As long as the word tickles their ears you will be safe, but when it pricks their heart, you are in danger. Here are a couple of good quotes from Matthew Henry in regards to this chapter in Ezekiel.

> *There are many who take pleasure in hearing the word, but make no conscience of doing it, and so they build upon the sand and deceive themselves... Serious things should be spoken of seriously..*

We live in a society where "Christians" don't want God in their playtime. This is not real Christianity. There is an abnormal and unusual separation from the ways of the Lord. People have desired to leave a daily abiding, and have turned into double minded Christians. There is a misconception that "Social Time," and "Time with the Lord" need to have no connection; they are separate but I say, in agreement with the Word of God, that we are to

ABIDE in Christ in EVERYTHING, Always.

Many of the words that you speak, will come against this mentality, for many "so called" believers are living and lying in the bed of the world, and have no desire for the Highway of Holiness.

Our purpose on the wall is to help rescue people that are in sin, have been wounded, or are going the wrong way. Many of these people are drowning and they do not know it. Your job is to rescue them, from their ocean of sin, but this is not an easy task. If you have any knowledge about emergency rescues, they will tell you that when saving a drowning person, you are in great danger yourself. For the drowning person will most commonly fight back, even to the point of drowning you. Now they do teach you to punch them, and knock them out to save them if necessary, but I am saying that is strictly for the purposes of natural water rescue. In the spirit you must simply take warning that drowning people get aggressively violent at the ones who are trying to help the most. This is why fervent prayer and intercession are vital for your ministry of redemption.

If you have been walking in prophetic ministry for a long time chances are you have experienced this anger and violence towards your ministry of truth. After a long time walking on the wall with bullets flying at you from every direction, you can easily become "Shell Shocked" over time. The term Shell Shocked comes from men who fight in war, and because of the amount of fighting they have seen, small things trigger, larger violent reactions. They also worry about many circumstances and think the enemy is shooting at them from behind every bush. This is a perfect illustration as to what happens to many "Prophetic Christians". As watchmen we all can become shell shocked, and think everyone is out to get us. But we must be aware of this danger, and deal with it properly. If you are shell shocked or see someone who is, we must tell them, and help restore them. Otherwise their ministry for the Lord will be compromised, and many people will be neglected in the process. The best way to recover from being shell shocked is to return to an extended season with communion in the comfort of the Lord through the Word and prayer. But make no mistake, you can and will get back up onto the wall again.

The key to the battle that we stand and fight in, is our responses to all of the attacks that come at us. We see normal humans speaking such horrible things, yet they themselves are not the enemy. True they may be used by the enemy, but we must remember that God wants to redeem them from their darkness. It's about hating the devil, not hating the people used by the devil. If you can have a dart shot at you, and use your shield to deflect it, and then pray a prayer of blessing towards that person who shot it, you are walking in God's victory.

The final illustration before this chapter closes, is about Jesus. The victory in all of your battles prophetically is in the example of Jesus and in his responses to attacks. Jesus clearly demonstrated amazing steadfastness in all of his persecutions, ridicule, and abuse.

> *He was oppressed, and he was afflicted, yet he opened not his mouth; like a lamb that is led to the slaughter, and like a sheep that before its shearers is silent, so he opened not his mouth.*
>
> *Isaiah 53:7*

This is a wonderful picture of how Jesus responded to persecutions, this does not mean however that Jesus did not speak or address problems when directed by the Holy Spirit. But as scripture prophesied he had no need to retaliate even in the midst of the most severe persecution any man suffered. They hit him, he stood still. They spit on him; he did not spit back. They grabbed his beard, and pulled out serious chunks of it, and he did not lash back at them. They put a crown of thorns on his head, and he did not hit them back. Jesus was not wrong in anything he did, and he had every right on earth and in heaven to destroy everyone who persecuted him, yet he remained like a lamb to the slaughter.

Jesus is our ultimate example of responding to unrighteous attacks. As you walk your journey as a watchman you will come under the same attacks in this dark age. If you want to be a successful minister you must have this settled in your heart now, " I will not, and cannot retaliate even if I am in the right!" As the arrows fly your direction you must be able to pray a prayer of redemption for the one who shot it. Without a doubt we know that Jesus prayed even for those who persecuted him. We must take his supreme example and apply it to our ministry as well. Yet even Jesus knew how difficult the battle is, and he himself grieved over the turmoil of it.

There is a real war going on, and it is not an easy battle. There will be times when the battle is raging so thick while you are up on that wall fighting, that you will break into tears because of the intensity. It is ok to go ahead and cry out your heart to the Father, he will take your tears in a bottle and bring you comfort. The battle is thick and your position on the wall can cause extreme pain and sadness. But just remember that Jesus cried and sobbed to the Father because of the battle and cup ahead of him, and the persecution coming to him on the cross. But, he continued forward in the Lord and by the Holy Spirit, you can continue forward just like Jesus too.

Other times the persecution of people will be so great you may buckle under pressure, but remember that God put you in your position not man. Just because the place of battle, the Lord has called you to, is on a wall, does not mean that you are a high and lofty person. On the contrary, you are actually in one of the most vulnerable places of the battle. You can be hit from both sides. But many will look at you on that wall and say, "They are looking down upon us," thinking that you have made yourself judge over them. Do not give into the temptation of feeling wrong about your position. Stand your ground, blow that trumpet, and swing that sword of truth! For many in the process will be protected from the flaming darts of the enemy, and others will be healed where they are wounded, simply because you obeyed God, spoke His word, and stayed on the wall.

Your purpose is a ministry of pointing others towards the truth in a loving way, for the purposes of redemption. If Mr. Brown's shoe is untied, he needs to know. It is not a ministry of flashy cars, or expensive houses like some would think, it is a lonely road. It's not a billboard ministry, or a ministry of fame and glamour, it is a ministry of pain and suffering.

When you go from town to town, you won't have a limo taking you there from the airport. It's not a rags to riches ministry, rather it is a rags to sackcloth ministry. A true prophetic road is not a red carpet, pomp and circumstance kind of ministry where everyone loves you. It is a lonely road of sharp jagged rocks with no praise to your words, or thankfulness of your thoughts. It is a lonely road, but many have walked it before us. Truly indeed the only crowd that follows a true prophet is the crowd of haters, and persecutors. Our ministry is not welcome in many places, it is a very narrow path. However, it is not one that we can avoid, if indeed God has called you to walk in this part of the five fold ministry.

Stand, know God, and speak the truth in the love in the place God puts you. Do not be afraid of the ridicule or persecutions, but desire redemption at all costs, even of your own life. For God is with us, even in this deep battle.

> Behold, I have refined thee, but not with silver; I have chosen thee in the furnace of affliction...."
>
> Isaiah 48:10 (KJV)

> Then Nebuchadnezzar the king was astonied, and rose up in haste, and spake, and said unto his counsellors, Did not we cast three men bound into the midst of the fire? They answered and said unto the king, True, O king. He answered and said, Lo, I see four men loose, walking in the midst of the fire, and they have no hurt; and the form of the fourth is like the Son of God."
>
> Daniel 3:24-25 (KJV)

> Listen to me, you who know right from wrong, you who cherish my law in your hearts. Do not be afraid of people's scorn, nor fear their insults.
>
> Isaiah 51:7 (KJV)

Who, when he was reviled, reviled not again; when he suffered, he threatened not; but committed himself to him that judgeth righteously...

1 Peter 2:23 (KJV)

Your guard in the attacks, is the Lord Jesus Christ at your side. If you walk with him, in his ways, using his words, you will be protected completely. Do not step out from under the guiding of the Holy Spirit. But you must fight this unseen battle for truth, and penetrate the darkness with it. Praise the Lord when you walk with other brothers and sisters in this process also, for they will be a great ministry from the hands of the Lord for you. Be strong and of good courage! Don't sit down, don't give up, for there are lives at stake, and everyone has a position in the body of Christ, some on the wall of a Watchman.

Though darts of destruction may come from the outside, and arrows of accusation may fly from the inside, let your declaration to the enemy be this: If I perish, I perish, but I will NOT come down off this wall!

CHAPTER FIFTEEN

Displaying Your Colors

We saw in Chapter 13 that there was a battle to prevent you from taking your position in the Body of Christ. We also saw in Chapter 14, that there is fire at you while you are in your position on the wall. Now in this chapter we will discuss another danger towards Prophetic Ministry, and this is a different kind of attack. This attack will try and come at you in a "deceptive" way of "Good Will" mixed with "Flattery". The whole purpose of this attack is to get you to leave the wall and fight battles that are not yours to fight. The victory in this is by always displaying your colors in Prophetic Ministry, and most of these deceptive "Silver Platters" will be tossed by the wayside.

In this chapter we are going to discuss 4 words that begin with the letter "R". Two of these words are good (Reformation & Restoration), and 2 are bad (Revolution & Revolt). I will briefly define these for you now, and then continue the discussion in the chapter. Though this will not be a long chapter, it is still very important for you to know while you walk in prophetic ministry. Because if you walk in the dark in regards to these words, you can and will be in danger.

Reformation & Reform (Added For Emphasis)... "The act of reforming; correction or amendment of life, manners, or of anything vicious or corrupt; as the reformation of manners; reformation of the age; reformation of abuses.

Reform... To change from worse to better; to amend; to correct; to restore to a former good state, or to bring from a bad to a good state; as, to reform a profligate man; to reform corrupt manners or morals."

Restoration... "Renewal; revival; re-establishment; as the restoration of friendship between enemies; the restoration of peace after war; the restoration of a declining commerce. Recovery; renewal of health and soundness; as restoration from sickness or from insanity. Recovery from a lapse or any bad state; as the restoration of man from apostasy. In theology, universal restoration, the final recovery of all men from sin and alienation from God, to a state of happiness;"

Revolution... "The overthrow or renunciation of one ruler or government and substitution of another by the governed."

Revolt... "To fall off or turn from one to another. To renounce allegiance and subjection to one's prince or state; to reject the authority of a sovereign; as a province or a number of people. To turn; to put to flight; to overturn. To shock; to do violence to; to cause to shrink or turn away with abhorrence; as, to revolt the mind or the feelings. Desertion; change of sides; more correctly, a renunciation of allegiance and subjection to one's prince or government; as the revolt of a province of the Roman empire. Gross departure from duty."

We live in a world where everything is falling apart, and many people and civilizations are on the verge of collapse. Revolution, revolt, and the likes there of are very commonly found in the mouths of people today. In our own Western World, we have new Independent Parties, Tea Parties, Non-Conformists, Conspiracy Theorist, and plenty of other people who simply hate the government. This chapter is written to warn you of some of these groups, and to caution you about anyone who comes to you to lead you away from the task God has given you of Redemption. Now I am not saying that these groups of people are bad in themselves, but it is important to express caution, and wisdom in your associations. Let's take a look at some scriptures and some modern day examples of Good Reforming, and Bad Revolting, and let us learn from them well before we start our ministry.

First let's talk about what Real Good Reformation looks like. The first example is of King Josiah. When Josiah became King of Judah, he was very young, but when he got older, his reforms started almost immediately. Some of the first things that were removed were the high places, and the pagan shrines. Josiah did not stop until the idols were broken into pieces. Later in his life however there was still plenty to have been done, but laxity fell upon him and the original mission of reformation dwindled. That is until Hilkiah the priest found the Book of Law in the house of the Lord. Interestingly enough the words in the book scared many of them and warned of coming wrath from the Lord. This highly motivated Josiah to finish the reformations that he had left undone. We follow the account of this at 2 Chronicles 34.

> *Then the king sent and gathered together all the elders of Judah and Jerusalem. And the king went up to the house of the LORD, with all the men of Judah and the inhabitants of Jerusalem and the priests and the Levites, all the people both great and small.*

> *And he read in their hearing all the words of the Book of the Covenant that had been found in the house of the LORD. And the king stood in his place and made a covenant before the LORD, to walk after the LORD and to keep his commandments and his testimonies and his statutes, with all his heart and all his soul, to perform the words of the covenant that were written in this book. Then he made*

all who were present in Jerusalem and in Benjamin join in it. And the inhabitants of Jerusalem did according to the covenant of God, the God of their fathers. And Josiah took away all the abominations from all the territory that belonged to the people of Israel and made all who were present in Israel serve the LORD their God. All his days they did not turn away from following the LORD, the God of their fathers.

2 Chronicles 34:29-33

King Josiah did more than most of the Kings of Judah and Israel, yet he still needed to remember what God's intentions were for his children. God did not in any way want his children to be caught up in idol worship, or high places. It was good that the fear of the Lord once again came upon King Josiah to finish the work he had started. The sad reality is that most of the other kings did not care about reformation, and left many of the high places in tack. This we can gather by reading these very commonly written statements that appear numerous times in the books of Kings & Chronicles. Here is one instance below.

Nevertheless, the high places were not taken away. The people still sacrificed and made offerings on the high places.

2 Kings 15:4

Nevertheless Josiah still did what was right in the eyes of the Lord, he had a Good Heart of Reformation, and the Lord delighted in him. For the next story lets move on and briefly take a look at another Old Testament example of a Bad Revolt, instead of redemption. Let's look at the life of Moses before he encountered God. We will pick up this story in Exodus 2.

One day, when Moses had grown up, he went out to his

people and looked on their burdens, and he saw an Egyptian
beating a Hebrew, one of his people. He looked this way and
that, and seeing no one, he struck down the Egyptian and
hid him in the sand. When he went out the next day, behold,
two Hebrews were struggling together. And he said to the
man in the wrong, "Why do you strike your companion?" He
answered, "Who made you a prince and a judge over us? Do
you mean to kill me as you killed the Egyptian?" Then Moses
was afraid, and thought, "Surely the thing is known."When
Pharaoh heard of it, he sought to kill Moses. But Moses fled
from Pharaoh and stayed in the land of Midian."

Exodus 2:11-15

Even though the Egyptian Leader was wrong for beating the Hebrew Slave, he was still in charge in that scenario. Yet Moses took it into his own hands to revolt against the injustice and bring the outcome a different way. Yes, the slave being beaten was unfair, unjust, and ruthless, yet the Egyptian's were still in charge. Moses saw the unfair treatment, and defended this Hebrew in "his" opinion of justice. Even though Moses was Right for what he saw, he was wrong in his manner of response to the matter. Death, retaliation, or any form of violence as justice, in our hands is never a right form of reformation. If your flesh produces the fruit of unrighteousness, you will be like Moses, before God got a hold of his heart, and hands.

It is easy for us to see Biblical examples of "Reformation" in the Old Testament as violent, or extreme. But we no longer live in the Old Testament Age, we are now walking in the New Covenant Age, and our prophetic ministry must walk in a new way. It is important to remind you that the Old Testament is types and shadows of the New Covenant, and that we no longer have to fight against flesh and blood, but against darkness and principalities in the heavenly places. Our new journey is a Spiritual Battle, the prophets of Old walked in a Physical Battle. To recap, Josiah reformed with Redemption in Mind, but Moses Revolted with

Fleshly Justice in Mind.

For the next example of potential Revolt, let's look at what happened to Jesus in the Book of John. In Chapter 6 we see the great miracle that Jesus did when he fed the 5000 people. It wasn't long after this that we see the heart of the people come out. The story will pick up in John chapter 6.

> *Jesus then took the loaves, and when he had given thanks, he distributed them to those who were seated. So also the fish, as much as they wanted. And when they had eaten their fill, he told his disciples, "Gather up the leftover fragments, that nothing may be lost." So they gathered them up and filled twelve baskets with fragments from the five barley loaves left by those who had eaten. When the people saw the sign that he had done, they said, "This is indeed the Prophet who is to come into the world!" Perceiving then that they were about to come and take him by force to make him king, Jesus withdrew again to the mountain by himself.*
>
> *John 6:11-15*

Throughout history the Jews have suffered oppression and suppression by others. In Jesus' day the Jews were no longer under Egyptian oppression, but Roman oppression and rule. They knew the Old Testament prophecies and anxiously awaited for their King and Messiah to come. They thought that this "Messiah" was to overthrow the government and lead them out of their physical oppression and bondage, much like with Moses. Simply put they were waiting for a "Revolution" to happen. As we see in the above passage Jesus had just fed 5000 people, and the people loved him for this miracle. They realized that he was "The Prophet" that the scriptures spoke of, and they tried to force him into "Kingship" before his appointed time. Instead Jesus refused this approach and quickly removed himself from the mob of revolutionaries. He had the Cross in the forefront of his mind, for it would be on that cross that true redemption for the people could actually come.

These people were not wrong for wanting a new king so that change could come, but they could not see the Big Picture of redemption. If Jesus would have joined, or allowed them to make him physical King, he would have never gone to the cross, and there would be no redemption available to them, and us. Though their intentions may have seemed good, they were actually getting in the way of God's great plan of Salvation. The same is for the Revolutionist. They are not wrong for wanting to bring change, but they are wrong for how they want to bring that change. They must realize that redemption must always be in mind, and that you cannot force "IN" the Kingdom of God, or Reformation by fleshly means.

The next aspect of Reformation that is necessary to briefly talk about is from our modern years. Let's briefly talk about the Reformation of Martin Luther, and William Wilberforce. In bringing out these two individuals we also see the clear tactics of those who have an agenda of Revolution instead of pure Reformation. I was very impressed with the stories and biographies of these two individuals in history. I totally agree with many that the lives of these men were not flawless and a bed of roses, yet none-the-less there was much good fruit that came from their passion for truth. In recent years I viewed documentary/dramatized films on these men's lives. Now whether or not these films are identical to the actual history of their lives I do not know, but there are two great illustrations from both biographies that I would like to use to make this topic clear. Let's begin first with the story of Martin Luther.

When Martin Luther came on the scene the Catholic Church was in financial and ethical collapse. Martin Luther left his monastery to study in a school of theology. His spiritual father in the monastery knew that he had a good mind to learn, and a good heart for change. Once at the school of theology, Martin showed his intellectual power, and came upon the blunt awful reality of the Catholic Church.

Using evil tactics of "Indulgences" and wicked character the Catholic Church caused Martin Luther to start the first real Reformation in the 1500's. However many believe that a close teacher of Martin joined this reformation with the wrong intentions. This teacher started a very dogmatic and open revolt against everything in the Catholic Church. This caused riots, revolts, and death. It was not Luther's intentions of revolt, but good did come eventually, because we believe God works out all things to the good. This teacher formed a "people's party" and this became more of a social revolt instead of a Religious Reformation. Luther did step in and help smooth over some of the riots, yet not all, and this teacher was kicked out of town by him. So the story goes.

For the next story let's talk about William Wilberforce and his intentions to abolish slave trade in England. William was a wealthy young man, with a great intellectual mouth both for studies and for singing. He was influential in politics, and rose to great power in the parliament of England with his close friend. During this time Wilberforce was highly influential with many good humanitarian acts. A group of activists came to influence him about slavery, and he was convinced about its evil nature. This became his agenda for the next several years. He fought long and hard to see slavery be abolished, while England was at war. However, the money earned by the slave owners and the men of parliament proved to hinder his bill for ending slave trade. After many years of trying and failing, it seemed this bill would never pass. Positioned in a place of authority and power, Wilberforce was approached by an itinerate minister who tried to influence him by comparing England's struggles to that of France. This minister came to him and spoke the word Revolution. This minister gave up on gentle reformations, and insisted upon forceful corrections. At once without blinking an eye, Wilberforce looked at this pastor and said, "You will never mention Revolution in my presence again." They parted ways for many seasons. Wilberforce did not want to revolt against the corrupt Parliament, but try and reform it from within, using peaceable tactics. This represents a man of dignity and honor, to which we should be influenced by, in our ministry, and purpose. These men were used in a mighty way for the Lord, yet the tactics of the devil came very close to them, attempting to pull them off course.

Reformation, and Revolution are drastically different and we must know the difference when people are trying to influence our lives. Let's bring this chapter to a conclusion by looking at the following thoughts.

Your position on a wall as a prophetic watchman is of utter importance and dedication. If the devil can't kill you, he will try and woo you off the wall into a task separate from what God gives you to do. Many people of seemingly "Good Will" will come to you trying to draw your attention to other "legitimate issues". Not all of these will be legitimate, but if you are to be faithful to your call then you must not be moved by anything other than God. You could be focused on a certain edification in the body, and someone could come drawing your eyes to another breach in the wall. If you take your eyes off of the task that is in front of you, your objective will be compromised. Just like I cautioned you to be careful with people who want to chew on bones, so to in this chapter I wish to caution you to be mindful of people who might have other hidden agendas.

If you are walking in the Spirit of God people will see the power of the Lord flowing through you. Many times these people who have hidden agendas of "Revolt" will try and use you for their purposes. You must be very cautious if someone tries to quickly bring you to action. The peace of God must be ruling in your heart before any direction change. People who wish to talk conspiracies, or against government officials all the time, reflect a lack of character and trust in God. These people would love to use a "Spirit Filled Prophet" to bring their agenda, or revolution to pass. The mind set of revolutionist is never truly founded in redemption and restoration, and this is why we must notably display our colors in what we stand for. Once you know their colors, it will be important for you to withdraw.

As was said earlier in a previous chapter, we must always respect and be mindful of the authorities that God has placed over us. Our victory as Christians is not the overthrowing of a bad government, or authority, it is in peaceable prayer and petitions to God. The same goes in the church body, and we must see the Redemption capability in a church instead of its split and demise. If you start attending a church with serious problems, reformation is ok to go after. But don't be too quick to react to the problems that you see. Make sure the peace of the Lord has been grounded in your heart, and that you are rooted in redemptive prayer.

I say emphatically that there is a massive need for Reformation in the church body today. But this will not be accomplished by revolting against leadership, or forming an uprising against their failures. It first starts in the prayer closet, then it moves to your mouth, then life will come forth. Reformation, and restoration go hand in hand with redemption and love. If the truth that you see, cannot pour forth with Heavenly LOVE, your words are banging cymbals and gongs. Even still I redundantly say, reformation needs to come to the church today.

God is not looking for people to join an army of revolt, but looking for a body to join arms in restoration. The devil, the world, much of society, and many in the church would prefer you to stay silent and get off the wall. These dangers come against you with sheer force and intimidation, but you must not give up. It is so important for you to Display your Colors of Reformation, lest people think they can join you in "revolt". If your true colors are not on display many will think of you potentially as dangerous. There are many of us who have experienced the dangers of people seeing our colors wrongly. Furthermore even if people see your colors correctly they may despise you, because they don't see any problems in their midst. Even these are dangers to your ministry, those who deny the need for Reformation. We must always show our colors plainly, and those colors are the colors of Redemption, Restoration, and Reformation. Make no mistake, we should not come down off the wall, because there is much work to be done.

So what does modern Reformation actually look like for us today in the church Body? The answer is simple, "The foolishness of preaching... The Truth!

Though being warned about the dangers...

Don't be afraid of them...

Your victory in Christ Jesus is sure!"

Section 4

Anointed Eyes
Seeing the Big Picture

*It's not about seeing the problem,
it's about seeing the answer to the problem!*

CHAPTER SIXTEEN

Lovers of Truth vs.
Lovers of Lawlessness

In this final section, I will now discuss some of the most exciting realities of the prophetic journey. That is "Seeing the Big Picture with Anointed Eyes"! Many times we walk down this narrow path and we strain to see things ahead of us, but to close this book we must stop for a moment in this final section and look at the larger picture of Redemption. If we only walk with our eyes to our feet, we will often miss the bigger picture God has set before us, and our purpose in the body. It is one thing to speak with an Anointed Tongue, but it is a far greater thing to see clearly with the eyes of Jesus to the matters at hand. God is on a course of redemption, and we must grasp that, while we walk this narrow path. The devil is also on a course; the course of war and destruction, and we must be aware of his tactics in the process. If you pay attention to what the devil is doing first, your prophetic journey will be filled with fear and tension. But if you are communing with the Lord Jesus first, your eyes will become anointed, thus giving you the peace to walk through the valley of the shadow of death. It is by having deep communion with the Lord, that you will walk out your ministry with Anointed Eyes. Having these anointed eyes will cause you to see redemption in all situations. These eyes will also guard you in the process to the ways of the devil.

In this chapter we will discuss the difference between truth and lawlessness. We live in the end times most notably, and truth is far from a reality in many social, and religious settings. The whole purpose in this chapter is to reveal God's Truth, and to expose the devil's lawlessness. It is vital to define the truth of the Bible as Absolute Truth in this chapter, and to define lawlessness as moral relativism. It is easy to identify lawlessness because it is anything besides truth and the character of God. Simply put, this topic is a black or white topic and there is no middle ground, neither can gray areas be an option. Let's begin by defining absolute truth, by definitions, and by verses from Scripture.

1st Section: Truth, and the Lovers of Truth... Absolute Truth

Truth (As Defined in Webster's 1828 Dictionary... "Conformity to fact or reality; exact accordance with that which is, or has been, or shall be. true state of facts or things. The duty of a court of justice is to discover the truth. Witnesses are sworn to declare the truth, the whole truth, and nothing but the truth. Conformity of words to thoughts, which is called moral truth. Veracity; purity from falsehood; practice of speaking truth; habitual disposition to speak truth; as when we say, a man is a man of truth. Correct opinion. Fidelity; constancy. Honesty; virtue. Exactness; conformity to rule. Real fact of just principle; real state of things."

Absolute (As in Webster's... "Literally, in a general sense, free, independent of any thing extraneous. Hence, Complete in itself; positive; as an absolute declaration."

Therefore Absolute Truth (my definition) is...Complete Truth, without error, undeniably, pure, right, moral, honest and good. Unable to be broken, or changed by the thoughts of man or philosophy. Stands alone under the persecution of man over time.

Now let's take a look at several verses from scripture about Truth, and what it looks like to God.

> *Jesus said to him, "I am the way, and the truth, and the life. No one comes to the Father except through me.*
>
> *John 14:6*

> *Jesus answered, "You say that I am a king. For this purpose I was born and for this purpose I have come into the world—to bear witness to the truth. Everyone who is of the truth listens to my voice.*
>
> *John 18:37*

> *Sanctify them in the truth; your word is truth.*
>
> *John 17:17*

> *But the hour is coming, and is now here, when the true worshipers will worship the Father in spirit and truth, for the Father is seeking such people to worship him. God is spirit, and those who worship him must worship in spirit and truth.*
>
> *John 4:23-24*

> *Make me to know your ways, O LORD; teach me your paths. Lead me in your truth and teach me, for you are the God of my salvation; for you I wait all the day long.*
>
> *Psalms 25:4-5*

> *Send out your light and your truth; let them lead me; let them bring me to your holy hill and to your dwelling!*
>
> *Psalms 43:3*

> *Behold, you delight in truth in the inward being, and you teach me wisdom in the secret heart.*
>
> *Psalms 51:6*

Thy word is true from the beginning: and every one of thy righteous judgments endureth forever.

Psalms 119:160 (KJV)

Buy the truth, and sell it not; also wisdom, and instruction, and understanding.

Proverbs 23:23

Therefore looking at all of these verses we can ask the question, "What is Truth? The answer is the Word of God. The next question is, "Who is the Word of God and Truth? The answer is Jesus. Jesus is the complete truth, being sent to us from God to manifest the plan of Salvation to a fallen people. All truth is founded in Jesus. The word of God is totally true, every word that comes from it, the mouth of Jesus, and God's inspired scribes is 100% true. The Bible is in reality, "Absolute Truth".

So Absolute Truth from the Christian perspective can be summed up as: Jesus Christ! This is a statement of fact with which we cannot debate.. It is a reality of truth that cannot change or be destroyed. A cornerstone or foundation that is not weak. When the "Vote" comes in it is not something that can be proven wrong in any way. It is a law of utter importance, immovable, not based on human logic or understanding. "In the Beginning was the Word." The Truth of God, the Truth of Jesus, the Truth of the Holy Spirit, and the Truth of his Written Word is the standard by which all other things are judged accordingly. God's word and God's throne are immovable, God is All Truth!

2nd Section: Lawlessness, Lovers of Lawlessness, Moral Relativism

Lawlessness (From Webster's)... "The quality or state of being unrestrained by law; disorder."

Moral Relativism: "Subjective reasoning that determines what is right or wrong in one's own eyes. All aspects of truth molds to one's own personal constitution. Whatever seems right for each person in each situation, as determined by each one's choices."

Rebellion... "An open and avowed renunciation of the authority of the government to which one owes allegiance; or the taking of arms traitorously to resist the authority of lawful government; revolt. Rebellion differs from insurrection and from mutiny. Insurrection may be a rising in opposition to a particular act or law, without a design to renounce wholly all subjection to the government. Insurrection may be, but is not necessarily, rebellion. Mutiny is an insurrection of soldiers or seamen against the authority of their officers. Open resistance to lawful authority."

Now let's look at several verses from scripture about the idea of living lawlessly. And of course the beginning of lawlessness as has already been stated in a previous chapter begins with the devil, and his sinful choice.

> *You are of your father the devil, and your will is to do your father's desires. He was a murderer from the beginning, and does not stand in the truth, because there is no truth in him. When he lies, he speaks out of his own character, for he is a liar and the father of lies."*
> *John 8:44*

> *Therefore God gave them up in the lusts of their hearts to impurity, to the dishonoring of their bodies among themselves, because they exchanged the truth about God for a lie and worshiped and served the creature rather than the Creator, who is blessed forever! Amen.*
> *Romans 1:24-25*

> *...but for those who are self-seeking and do not obey the truth, but obey unrighteousness, there will be wrath and fury.*
> *Romans 2:8*

Now concerning the coming of our Lord Jesus Christ and our being gathered together to him, we ask you, brothers, not to be quickly shaken in mind or alarmed, either by a spirit or a spoken word, or a letter seeming to be from us, to the effect that the day of the Lord has come. Let no one deceive you in any way. For that day will not come, unless the rebellion comes first, and the man of lawlessness is revealed, the son of destruction, who opposes and exalts himself against every so-called god or object of worship, so that he takes his seat in the temple of God, proclaiming himself to be God. Do you not remember that when I was still with you I told you these things? And you know what is restraining him now so that he may be revealed in his time.

For the mystery of lawlessness is already at work. Only he who now restrains it will do so until he is out of the way. And then the lawless one will be revealed, whom the Lord Jesus will kill with the breath of his mouth and bring to nothing by the appearance of his coming. The coming of the lawless one is by the activity of Satan with all power and false signs and wonders, and with all wicked deception for those who are perishing, because they refused to love the truth and so be saved. Therefore God sends them a strong delusion, so that they may believe what is false, in order that all may be condemned who did not believe the truth but had pleasure in unrighteousness. But we ought always to give thanks to God for you, brothers beloved by the Lord, because God chose you as the firstfruits to be saved, through sanctification by the Spirit and belief in the truth. To this he called you through our gospel, so that you may obtain the glory of our Lord Jesus Christ. So then, brothers, stand firm and hold to the traditions that you were taught by us, either by our spoken word or by our letter. Now may our Lord Jesus Christ himself, and God our Father, who loved us and gave us eternal comfort and good hope through grace, comfort your hearts and establish them in every good work and word.

2 Thessalonians 2:1-17

And you shall say to them, 'This is the nation that did not obey the voice of the LORD their God, and did not accept discipline; truth has perished; it is cut off from their lips.
Jeremiah 7:28

But understand this, that in the last days there will come times of difficulty. For people will be lovers of self, lovers of money, proud, arrogant, abusive, disobedient to their parents, ungrateful, unholy, heartless, unappeasable, slanderous, without self-control, brutal, not loving good, treacherous, reckless, swollen with conceit, lovers of pleasure rather than lovers of God, having the appearance of godliness, but denying its power. Avoid such people.
2 Timothy 3:1-5

So in essence, "Lawlessness" can be summed up this way: "Doing what is right in your own eyes and forming your own personal opinions around how you feel." There is no real law and order in the universe or society, and no one can make you hold to any real form of truth or law. Furthermore lawlessness is also a clear form of rebellion, and rebellion is a clear form of witchcraft, and witchcraft is of the devil. It can also be said in another way...

For although they knew God, they did not honor him as God or give thanks to him, but they became futile in their thinking, and their foolish hearts were darkened. Claiming to be wise, they became fools, and exchanged the glory of the immortal God for images resembling mortal man and birds and animals and creeping things. Therefore God gave them up in the lusts of their hearts to impurity, to the dishonoring of their bodies among themselves, because they exchanged the truth about God for a lie and worshiped and served the creature rather than the Creator, who is blessed forever! Amen. For this reason God gave them up to dishonorable passions. For their women exchanged natural relations for those that are contrary to nature; and the men likewise gave up natural relations with women and were consumed with passion for one another, men committing shameless acts with men and receiving in themselves the due penalty for their error. And since they did not see fit to acknowledge God, God gave them up to a debased mind to do what ought not to be done. They were filled with all manner of unrighteousness, evil, covetousness, malice. They are full of envy, murder, strife, deceit, maliciousness. They are gossips, slanderers, haters of God, insolent, haughty, boastful, inventors of evil, disobedient to parents, foolish, faithless, heartless, ruthless. Though they know God's righteous decree that those who practice such things deserve to die, they not only do them but give approval to those who practice them.

Romans 1:21-32

The bottom line is that, lawless people only want truth when it best suits them, and anything else that doesn't benefit them they call a "lie". Instead of conforming to the truth they rebel against it, write it off, and create another "truth" in their own mind. So in the name of tolerance there is actually "NO TOLERANCE" for real truth. Simply put anyone who wants to walk in a lawless way, must first deny a truth that originally and clearly exists. Lawlessness is the end result of denying God, and walking away from His clear truth set before us in; nature, by preaching, in the word, in the Life of Jesus Christ, in the wooing of the Holy Spirit, and through the free gift of God! No one can say that God has given up on mankind and not tried to reach out to them through grace. Yet the lawless one refuses to accept the truth of God, and thus turns away from that free gift of Jesus into a futile and rebellious end.

Now that we have the defining terms for these two categories, and scriptural references to what they look like, let's sum these two up before we move on, in this way; There are two camps of thinking, Absolute Truth vs. Lawlessness. In the Christian journey there is only one road of correct thinking to walk down, and that is the path of Absolute Truth. Either you believe the Word of God completely or you don't. If you do not, then you are walking in the camp of lawlessness.

It may not look like it to other Christians, or even to yourself, but if you devalue ANY of the Word's from God's Scripture in the slightest, you are starting to think in a lawless manner. It is a world view perspective, and you must choose wisely. Either you love and adore God's words to the fullest or you don't, there is no gray area. Those who pick and choose verses of scripture to take out at their leisure are demonstrating that they are rebellious, and lawlessness is at work in their hearts. We can not select one portion of scripture at the exclusion of another; we must remember to love and cherish His word, and walk it out by the Holy Spirit. It is simply black or white.

> *God's truth is absolute, but sometimes it becomes relative to us. We consider what we can do as truth, and what we dislike to keep as non-essential. We instead of God, evaluate the worth of truth. It becomes a matter of man controlling truth instead of truth controlling man.*
>
> *Watchman Nee*

So what does a Christian look like who believes in absolute truth? Well to do this we must travel back in history almost 2000 years to look at what a normal Christian life was in Rome. First let's look at Rome in its place as a world leader during the time of Jesus.

Rome was the world power, full of filth, immorality, greed, licentiousness, lusts of power, was strong in military, and had numerous pagan religions and cult worship. Then Jesus came into the equation speaking truth and with authority. To a society who knew nothing of truth, this was scandalous. However the Jews really didn't matter to Rome, because they were so small, insignificant, and easily conquered. Everyone did what was right in their own eyes, and no one really believed in anything but selfish pleasures and vain glory. Lawlessness was everywhere yet Rome maintained military control over it. We know truth was not a reality, by listening to Pilate when he spoke to Jesus and said the following.

> *Then Pilate said to him, "So you are a king?" Jesus answered, "You say that I am a king. For this purpose I was born and for this purpose I have come into the world— to bear witness to the truth. Everyone who is of the truth*

listens to my voice." Pilate said to him, "What is truth?

John 18:37–38

Coming from one of the key leaders of the day, one would think the world power knew all, and had ultimate truth. Yet a society that makes gods out of men does not really know truth at all. After Jesus was killed, those who believed in him became Christians, and these Christians knew the power of truth. However in ancient Roman history there were many religions in the land and the government. In fact many of them were combining together to form one national religion, the religion of Rome.

However this proved to be a problem for the Christians, because the Christians did not want to align themselves with these other pagan religions.

This is the reason why the Christians were persecuted in Rome. They were persecuted not necessarily because they were Christians, but because they started to rebel against the combining of these pagan religions into one religion. The Christians were not in any way going to accept this horrid thought of multi-god worship. They also refused to worship Caesar as a god before God. If they would have worshipped Caesar and God, they would have lived, because Rome was a very religious place with many worshipping in other cult religions. But Christians refused to worship Caesar and God, so they rebelled against it and stood alone, thus bringing a great and severe persecution. (Paraphrased from Francis Shaeffer's book, How Should We Then Live and his video series by the same name).

These Christians had a right world view. They believed in Jesus Christ, and believed in his Absolute Truth. Because they believed this, and refused to conform to the state's religious opinions they appeared on the radar as Rebellious to Rome. The people in the other religions were not killed as martyrs, because they recognized Caesar as god. The Christians held fast to Absolute Truth based upon the Word of God and walked out their destiny into the den of lions. This is what it looks like to walk in the ways of Absolute Truth, and not be afraid of the outcome.

The next question that comes is what does it look like to live in lawlessness? To answer this question we must fast forward 2000 years to our current society to grasp this reality. Unfortunately western American/European culture best illustrates this sad reality for us.

Hang on tight; in this next paragraph it is necessary to paint the desolate picture of America for you as a lawless land and nation. Lawlessness has swept over our morals and nation at rapid rates that none can deny. For example; The pornography industry makes more money in a year than ALL of the major sporting events do combined. Sex slave trade is the worst in the country through Atlanta, Georgia, the near center of the "Bible Belt". There are entire "Christian Denominations" ordaining sexually degenerated people as ministers and calling it biblical. Child Abusers have taken places of leadership in many Catholic Churches uncontested or exposed. The teenage suicide rate has massively increased to 1 out of every 13 kids. Drugs have moved from illegal on the streets to being openly prescribed through the pharmacies causing millions to be addicted to pain killers. School shootings, and senseless social shootings have increased at astronomical rates. Music, movies, and video games sell more when they are more violent. Finally, since 1973, there have been 54,559,615 abortions performed in America alone. This is not a chapter on the facts and stats of immorality; I could aimlessly go on for days without end. Do you get the picture of the status of American culture as lawlessness? If our status is this bad, and we call ourselves a "Christian Nation", think of the rest of the world who doesn't. We cannot call ourselves a "Christian Nation" in any way whatsoever.

Any nation that does not build entirely and solely upon "Christian Values" only; will fall into complete lawlessness. Rome was the exact same way before it fell and collapsed in moral, social, and political failure. We are exactly like Rome, if not abundantly worse. These problems start when society becomes a "Syncretistic" Society. So let's define Syncretism, and what it is to us today.

Syncretism... "Reconciliation or fusion of differing systems of belief, as in philosophy or religion, especially when success is partial or the result is heterogeneous. Or the combination of different beliefs: the combination of different systems of philosophical or religious belief or practice. Basically: The combining of various religions to serve a greater society purpose."

People become syncretistic when they walk away from Absolute Truth, and consider the Religion of the Land as more important than the Word of God. You may think that this cannot be so in America. You may think that religions are not being combined here, and that we are a Nation under God. With all do respect and courtesy it is important to prove to you otherwise by the following quote from one of our most recent so called "Christian" Presidents.

Taken From- "George W. Bush's Inauguration Speech 2005"

"....In America's ideal of freedom, the public interest depends on private character—on integrity, and tolerance toward others, and the rule of conscience in our own lives. Self-government relies, in the end, on the governing of the self. That edifice of character is built in families, supported by communities with standards, and sustained in our national life by the truths of Sinai, the Sermon on the Mount, the words of the Koran, and the varied faiths of our people. Americans move forward in every generation by reaffirming all that is good and true that came before—ideals of justice and conduct that are the same yesterday, today, and forever..."

There you have it ladies and gentlemen, Rome all over again. This is what happens when you move away from "Absolute Truth" to "Moral Relativism". When we do not depend wholly upon God's word, we step away from "Ultimate Truth" at rapid rates, and fall into "Political Correctness", and compromise. However to balance this equation I wish to say, I am incredibly thankful to be in America, and to have the freedom to worship God (at this time) without persecution. However many of us are not supportive of any society including our own that desires the people to move towards "Moral Relativism", which is "Lawlessness". Society has also crept into the church in this same manner which we have discussed in previous chapters.

The problem is that many so called "Christians" today are drinking from the cup of Truth on Sunday's and drinking from the cup of Compromise the rest of the week. The devil cannot stand absolute truth, this is why he has been twisting the truth from the very beginning. If he can get a Christian to question truth, then he puts them in the bondage of questioning everything, and soon that Christian will be a syncretistic Christian, and lose the love of truth in their life. Metaphorically speaking we cannot drink from the cup of the "World", and the cup of the Lord at the same time. Yet all the while it is not being said that you can't be in society, but rather it is being said that you must not become syncretistic. You must be careful while you are in the world not to misuse, over touch, or become joined with the immorality of the world.

The problem is, many "Christians" look like the "World". There should be no more confusion as to whether you are a Christian or not in today's society. You must look different, live different, and function different, yet you must remain in this world and not of it.

In this first chapter of "Seeing the Big Picture" I am deliberately suggesting to have your eyes opened to the reality of Truth and Lawlessness. Many people would call this Black or White stance as "Dogmatic" or "Legalistic", but the reality is, it's 100% Biblical. Because Scriptures says it plainly for us...

> *Do not love the world or the things in the world. If anyone loves the world, the love of the Father is not in him. For all that is in the world—the desires of the flesh and the desires of the eyes and pride of life—is not from the Father but is from the world. And the world is passing away along with its desires, but whoever does the will of God abides forever.*
>
> *1 John 2:15-17*

Truth tells us to avoid the desires of this world, yet lawlessness tells you that it is ok to partake, enjoy, and utilize this world at your subjection. Christianity and Lawlessness are polar opposite, and there can be no compromise between these two forces at work. If someone loves Truth at all costs it will be visible in their lives. If that person does not love truth, their lawlessness will come to surface eventually. The real road of Christianity, that is "TRUE CHRISTIANITY" is narrow.

> *Enter by the narrow gate. For the gate is wide and the way is easy that leads to destruction, and those who enter by it are many. For the gate is narrow and the way is hard that leads to life, and those who find it are few.*

> *Matthew 7:13-14*

If we are to walk as True Prophetic People we must be walking and speaking forth his absolute truth. If we walk otherwise and call ourselves God's people, we are simply hypocrites. It is for this reason that God's name has been blasphemed among the Gentiles. We must walk the straight and narrow path, speak the sharp, redeeming truth, while loving a lost and sinful humanity. Becoming like the world to reach the world never works, the greatest way we could ever relate to the world is by walking in Godliness. In doing so, they (the world) will come to grips with the reality that God is real, and that there is an Absolute Truth to live by. It is then their choice as to whether or not they will submit to Jesus Christ. The Christians during the latter time of Jesus had a choice to walk in the ways of Lawlessness, or to stand on Absolute Truth. If you look at the world through the anointed eyes of Jesus, you will see the difference between truth and lawlessness. Your ministry must be reflective of God's Absolute Truth, with no stench of Lawlessness in it.

Today we have this same choice once again as Christians, yet this time we cannot assume our destiny will be any different than the Christians in Rome. We must be willing to live a no compromise Christianity in the face of sheer persecution, and say with the rest of our cloud of faithful witnesses...

> *"I have decided to follow Jesus,*
> *no turning back, no turning back.*
> *The Cross before me,*
> *the world behind me,*
> *no turning back, no turning back!"*

CHAPTER SEVENTEEN

Moving from Knowledge to Life

Continuing in the theme of walking with "Anointed Eyes", let's venture diligently into this next chapter of great importance. This whole chapter reveals the importance of walking in the "Newness of Life", and not just knowledge. The theme is "Moving from Knowledge to Life", but we must first ask an important question. "Why are we moving from knowledge to life?"That question must be answered by revealing that God's original intention was life, and we transgressed that life into the knowledge of Good and Evil. This original hope of life was traded for knowledge of good and evil, in which it brought death to all humanity. Our prophetic ministry is a ministry of life, and if we walk in knowledge only, we will not be walking correctly in the heart of the Lord Jesus Christ. Let's begin by looking at where the great transgression started in the Garden of Eden.

The LORD God took the man and put him in the garden of
Eden to work it and keep it. And the LORD God commanded

the man, saying, "You may surely eat of every tree of the garden, but of the tree of the knowledge of good and evil you shall not eat, for in the day that you eat of it you shall surely die.

Genesis 2:15-17

Now the serpent was more crafty than any other beast of the field that the LORD God had made. He said to the woman, "Did God actually say, 'You shall not eat of any tree in the garden'?" And the woman said to the serpent, "We may eat of the fruit of the trees in the garden, but God said, 'You shall not eat of the fruit of the tree that is in the midst of the garden, neither shall you touch it, lest you die.'" But the serpent said to the woman, "You will not surely die.

For God knows that when you eat of it your eyes will be opened, and you will be like God, knowing good and evil." So when the woman saw that the tree was good for food, and that it was a delight to the eyes, and that the tree was to be desired to make one wise, she took of its fruit and ate, and she also gave some to her husband who was with her, and he ate. Then the eyes of both were opened, and they knew that they were naked. And they sewed fig leaves together and made themselves loincloths. And they heard the sound of the LORD God walking in the garden in the cool of the day, and the man and his wife hid themselves from the presence of the LORD God among the trees of the garden.

But the LORD God called to the man and said to him, "Where are you?" And he said, "I heard the sound of you in the garden, and I was afraid, because I was naked, and I hid myself." He said, "Who told you that you were naked? Have you eaten of the tree of which I commanded you not to eat?" The man said, "The woman whom you gave to be with me, she gave me fruit of the tree, and I ate." Then the LORD God said to the woman, "What is this that you have done?" The woman said, "The serpent deceived me, and I ate."

Genesis 3:1-13

Then the LORD God said, "Behold, the man has become like one of us in knowing good and evil. Now, lest he reach out his hand and take also of the tree of life and eat, and live forever."

Genesis 3:22-24

The perfect plan of the Lord as laid out in the garden was thwarted by the deceptions of the devil. The woman was deceived, then the man was deceived, then they both ate, and death entered the human race. The great chasm was built between man and God. For most of us we can only assume that before man fell, how wonderful it must have been walking in undivided fellowship with God. Yet the failure of mankind moved him into a fleshly, natural being, and tainting the purity that God had originally given him. It is in this garden that we see the same tactics the devil uses against us as Christians, and in prophetic ministry. But let's speak more of that later.

The reality is that man, as a result of the fall, walks, talks, and thinks in a worldly, and degenerated mind. Unless Jesus Christ saves a person, a person cannot produce life of any kind. This is the curse of the fall, and the result of sin. What I am trying to paint for you is this; "Our sinful Adamic nature produces knowledge and death, and there is an exceeding lust for this knowledge". Man lusts for knowledge for the wrong reason, because man wants POWER. Knowledge brings power whether for good or evil purposes. Our journey as Christians must move us from Knowledge to the Spirit Life! But to really see this illustrated for us, we must look at some relevant examples from scripture that shows us a life lived in Knowledge versus a life motivated by the Spirit.

The first and main example is looking deeper at the life of Paul before he was converted from Saul. In the chapter, "The Zeal of The Lord" the testimony of Paul was briefly mentioned, but in this chapter that testimony must be expanded to reveal the deeper aspect of being converted from Knowledge to life.

Let's look at several verses of scriptures to build this transition time in his life for us to consider further. The first few passages will be the actual historical accounts before and after his conversion, while the last few will be his own personal testimony of meeting Jesus Christ.

> Now when they heard these things they were enraged, and they ground their teeth at him. But he, full of the Holy Spirit, gazed into heaven and saw the glory of God, and Jesus standing at the right hand of God. And he said, "Behold, I see the heavens opened, and the Son of Man standing at the right hand of God." But they cried out with a loud voice and stopped their ears and rushed together at him. Then they cast him out of the city and stoned him. And the witnesses laid down their garments at the feet of a young man named Saul. And as they were stoning Stephen, he called out, "Lord Jesus, receive my spirit." And falling to his knees he cried out with a loud voice, "Lord, do not hold this sin against them." And when he had said this, he fell asleep.
>
> *Acts 7:54-60*

> And Saul approved of his execution. And there arose on that day a great persecution against the church in Jerusalem, and they were all scattered throughout the regions of Judea and Samaria, except the apostles. Devout men buried Stephen and made great lamentation over him. But Saul was ravaging the church, and entering house after house, he dragged off men and women and committed them to prison.
>
> *Acts 8:1-3*

But Saul, still breathing threats and murder against the disciples of the Lord, went to the high priest and asked him for letters to the synagogues at Damascus, so that if he found any belonging to the Way, men or women, he might bring them bound to Jerusalem. Now as he went on his way, he approached Damascus, and suddenly a light from heaven shone around him. And falling to the ground he heard a voice saying to him, "Saul, Saul, why are you persecuting me?" And he said, "Who are you, Lord?" And he said, "I am Jesus, whom you are persecuting. But rise and enter the city, and you will be told what you are to do." The men who were traveling with him stood speechless, hearing the voice but seeing no one. Saul rose from the ground, and although his eyes were opened, he saw nothing. So they led him by the hand and brought him into Damascus. And for three days he was without sight, and neither ate nor drank. Now there was a disciple at Damascus named Ananias. The Lord said to him in a vision, "Ananias." And he said, "Here I am, Lord."

And the Lord said to him, "Rise and go to the street called Straight, and at the house of Judas look for a man of Tarsus named Saul, for behold, he is praying, and he has seen in a vision a man named Ananias come in and lay his hands on him so that he might regain his sight." But Ananias answered, "Lord, I have heard from many about this man, how much evil he has done to your saints at Jerusalem. And here he has authority from the chief priests to bind all who call on your name." But the Lord said to him, "Go, for he is a chosen instrument of mine to carry my name before the Gentiles and kings and the children of Israel. For I will show him how much he must suffer for the sake of my name."So Ananias departed and entered the house. And laying his hands on him he said, "Brother Saul, the Lord Jesus who appeared to you on the road by which you came has sent me so that you may regain your sight and be filled with the Holy Spirit." And immediately something like scales fell from his eyes, and he regained his sight. Then he rose and was baptized; and taking food, he was strengthened. For some days he was with the disciples at Damascus. And immediately he proclaimed Jesus in the synagogues, saying, "He is the Son of God.

Acts 9:1-20

And all who heard him were amazed and said, "Is not this the man who made havoc in Jerusalem of those who called upon this name? And has he not come here for this purpose, to bring them bound before the chief priests?" But Saul increased all the more in strength, and confounded the Jews who lived in Damascus by proving that Jesus was the Christ. When many days had passed, the Jews plotted to kill him, but their plot became known to Saul. They were watching the gates day and night in order to kill him, but his disciples took him by night and let him down through an opening in the wall, lowering him in a basket. And when he had come to Jerusalem, he attempted to join the disciples. And they were all afraid of him, for they did not believe that he was a disciple.

But Barnabas took him and brought him to the apostles and declared to them how on the road he had seen the Lord, who spoke to him, and how at Damascus he had preached boldly in the name of Jesus. So he went in and out among them at Jerusalem, preaching boldly in the name of the Lord. And he spoke and disputed against the Hellenists. But they were seeking to kill him. And when the brothers learned this, they brought him down to Caesarea and sent him off to Tarsus.

Acts 9:21-30

End of the Historical Account, the following verses will be the actual testimony from Paul's own writings.

"I am a Jew, born in Tarsus in Cilicia, but brought up in this city, educated at the feet of Gamaliel according to the strict manner of the law of our fathers, being zealous for God as all of you are this day. I persecuted this Way to the death, binding and delivering to prison both men and women, as the high priest and the whole council of elders can bear me witness. From them I received letters to the brothers, and I journeyed toward Damascus to take those also who were there and bring them in bonds to Jerusalem to be punished. "As I was on my way and drew near to Damascus, about noon a great light from heaven suddenly shone around me. And I fell to the ground and heard a voice saying to me, 'Saul, Saul, why are you persecuting me?' And I answered, 'Who are you, Lord?' And he said to me, 'I am Jesus of Nazareth, whom you are persecuting.' Now those who were with me saw the light but did not understand the voice of the one who was speaking to me."

Acts 22:3-9

"Though I myself have reason for confidence in the flesh also. If anyone else thinks he has reason for confidence in the flesh, I have more: circumcised on the eighth day, of the people of Israel, of the tribe of Benjamin, a Hebrew of Hebrews; as to the law, a Pharisee; as to zeal, a persecutor of the church; as to righteousness under the law, blameless. But whatever gain I had, I counted as loss for the sake of Christ. Indeed, I count everything as loss because of the surpassing worth of knowing Christ Jesus my Lord. For his sake I have suffered the loss of all things and count them as rubbish, in order that I may gain Christ, that I may know him and the power of his resurrection, and may share his sufferings, becoming like him in his death..."

Philippians 3:4-10

For you have heard of my former life in Judaism, how I persecuted the church of God violently and tried to destroy it. And I was advancing in Judaism beyond many of my own age among my people, so extremely zealous was I for the traditions of my fathers. But when he who had set me apart before I was born, and who called me by his grace, was pleased to reveal his Son to me, in order that I might preach him among the Gentiles, I did not immediately consult with anyone; nor did I go up to Jerusalem to those who were apostles before me, but I went away into Arabia, and returned again to Damascus. Then after three years I went up to Jerusalem to visit Cephas and remained with him fifteen days. But I saw none of the other apostles except James the Lord's brother. (In what I am writing to you, before God, I do not lie!)

Then I went into the regions of Syria and Cilicia. And I was still unknown in person to the churches of Judea that are in Christ. They only were hearing it said, "He who used to persecute us is now preaching the faith he once tried to destroy. And they glorified God because of me."

Galatians 1:13-24

From the chapter on Zeal, and this chapter on Knowledge, we can easily gather that Paul had both of these traits visible and functioning in his life as a Pharisee. We see his incomplete Knowledge motivating his Zeal to action. There is no doubt that Paul knew the scriptures verbatim, he sat under the best teachers of Israel, and had permission to carry out his Zealous persecutions. Paul was truly full of knowledge and had a fervent desire for the traditions of his fathers. Yet this knowledge only led to persecution and death.

When Paul met Jesus on the roadside and encountered him for the first time, it was there that the seed of Life was implanted in his heart. At that point the knowledge that Paul thought he had was about to change for the rest of eternity. Paul spent his whole life (until that point) studying and growing in the ways of the Pharisees. Paul knew "Lots of stuff", but he didn't KNOW Jesus. However when he met Jesus he spent the next 15 years at least, having his entire "knowledge grid" reprogrammed into the "Real Life of Jesus". This real life of Jesus, produces real life in ministry. If your knowledge (like Paul's original knowledge) is based in traditions and the ways of man, people will not live as a result of your ministry. However, if your ministry is based in Jesus you will live, and others will live through your ministry.

Paul is an example of someone who functioned wrongly in a ministry based on "Knowledge" and not a ministry based on "Life". When God moved Paul from Knowledge to Life, his whole world changed, and real ministry began. For the next brief story let's take a look at the account of Martha and Jesus, to further dig into the topic of moving from Knowledge to life.

> *Then Jesus told them plainly, "Lazarus has died, and for your sake I am glad that I was not there, so that you may believe. But let us go to him." So Thomas, called the Twin, said to his fellow disciples, "Let us also go, that we may die with him." Now when Jesus came, he found that Lazarus had already been in the tomb four days.*

> *Bethany was near Jerusalem, about two miles off, and many of the Jews had come to Martha and Mary to console them concerning their brother. So when Martha heard that Jesus was coming, she went and met him, but Mary remained seated in the house. Martha said to Jesus, "Lord, if you had been here, my brother would not have died. But even now I know that whatever you ask from God, God will give you." Jesus said to her, "Your brother will rise again." Martha said to him, "I know that he will rise again in the resurrection on the last day." Jesus said to her, "I am the resurrection and the life. Whoever believes in me, though he die, yet shall he live, and*

everyone who lives and believes in me shall never die. Do you believe this?"She said to him, "Yes, Lord; I believe that you are the Christ, the Son of God, who is coming into the world.

John 11:14-27

The key verses which are important to bring out are:

Martha said to him, "I know that he will rise again in the resurrection on the last day." Jesus said to her, "I am the resurrection and the life. Whoever believes in me, though he die, yet shall he live, and everyone who lives and believes in me shall never die. Do you believe this?"

John 11:24-26

Martha states that, "I KNOW", yet Jesus actually questions her heart here. Jesus states that, "I am the resurrection and the Life". Martha had not yet experienced the Life giving power of Jesus. She thought she knew him, but it wasn't until he produced a LIFE giving experience before her eyes, that she was moved from Knowledge to Life. Martha is a perfect example of how many of us actually are as Christians. We hear the words of scripture, we listen to the words of preachers, we think we know the Life of God, and yet we often demonstrate a ministry of knowledge and not a ministry of life. To preach a message of life, you must be first experiencing this Life of Jesus for yourself, or it will just be knowledge you preach. I am not saying that you have to be dumb, and without knowledge in ministry. But rather, what is being said is this, knowledge without the life of Christ Jesus is a dangerous knowledge and has the potential to produce death rather than redemption. Let's take a closer look at knowledge to see the actions it produces as a result.

For example, if you see things prophetically about a matter you can say, "I have knowledge about this situation." You may have been given a word of knowledge about a particular breech in the wall of a church, but if you do not know the heart of the Lord about that breech, you may operate under knowledge only, and not life.

If you are quick to expose, rebuke, or broadcast this breech, you may indeed cause more damage than life. Just because you can see a matter with "knowledge" doesn't give you the immediate right to speak to a matter, or deal with it.

One of the tactics of the devil even from the very beginning of time was to cause man to pick knowledge over life. This same tactic is still being used against us today in the Body of Christ. The devil will often use these bating tactics to get us to see knowledge without seeing the redemption. Though we may see "partial" truths about a scenario, we must be founded on the complete truths from God's heart. He deceived Adam and Eve with the Lust of Knowledge, and mankind fell into death and destruction because of it. So we too will fall into death and destruction in our ministry if we bite the fruit of knowledge without drinking the cup of life. God's whole goal is to move us back from the Tree of Knowledge to the Tree of Life. Having the anointed eyes from the Lord will draw your heart away from the Knowledge Tree, to a tree that brings life.

One of the ways that you can grow into a life giving ministry, is by tempering your timing when speaking. Once again just because you can see something does not mean it is time for you to speak to a matter or address it. I have learned in my journey that God gives us 3 Tests as Prophets to perform before we speak. This is not founded necessarily in scripture, or in any other books, but I do see great wisdom in this approach to speaking. Therefore if you see something prophetically and have knowledge about a matter I believe first and foremost that God wants you to pray about that matter, and seek the heart of God in it. Secondly after doing this God will often instruct you in your own journey about that matter, to teach you, to protect you from doing the same, and to cause you to learn from it. Thirdly, if indeed God wants you to speak to a matter it is at this time when God may put the burden on your heart to confront a situation out of hand. But notice speaking to a matter is not always first. There are seasons when in a certain moment you must speak immediately to a situation, though I believe honestly this is an exception and is not the normality. Praying the heart of the Father, and learning from him, will instruct you when it is the right time to speak. In this moment, your words will be inspired by knowledge yet filled with life. The foundation is in Redeeming Life!

If you are walking with other fellow believers it will be easy to see and discern what type of ministry you are walking in. Do you rejoice over the flaws you find in other believers, or do you rejoice over their redemption from the flaws?

Though it is important to say emphatically, it is very easy at the beginning of any prophetic journey to start out harsh, sharp, and unloving. Many of us, (and I would be lying if I said otherwise) started out with a knowledge based ministry.

We are given gifts of foresight and discernment from the Lord, yet many of us don't know how to hold these instruments correctly. To paint this simply and clearly, the young prophet may look like a 10 year old boy trying to hold a fireman's hose at full blast. The water, hose, and young boy are being tossed around by the force and weight of something they cannot yet hold or maintain correctly. The young boy's actions are not wrong; he just has to grow in the strength of the Lord. Praise the Lord the boy is trying to put out a fire, yet he has to be tempered and trained correctly in the Lord. Who out there is willing to walk with young prophetic people while they learn these hard ropes to hold? To the mature in the Lord, you will do well to be loyal and faithful to these young men in the Lord who need proper instruction. To the young in the prophetic journey, God has given you a large responsibility to hold down, but don't lose heart, because God is capable of training you correctly in the right ways. If you will not heed the voice of the Spirit, or of legitimate wise authority, you will hurt someone in ministry, because your hose will swing out of control harming many in the process of putting out a fire.

As you continue to train and walk under the authority of the Lord, your ministry will not only see the "Fire" with Knowledge, but it will know how to put it out correctly and bring life again. We will always be tempted to lust for knowledge about someone, something, or some situation. If we take what we KNOW and turn it back to the Lord, he will then answer us with Life for that matter. The reality is that we must ask the Lord how to respond in that matter, and be faithful to wait for his answer. If we don't, we will look like the disciples in this following situation.

> *While he was still speaking, there came a crowd, and the man called Judas, one of the twelve, was leading them. He drew near to Jesus to kiss him, but Jesus said to him, "Judas, would you betray the Son of Man with a kiss?"*

> *And when those who were around him saw what would follow, they said,"Lord, shall we strike with the sword?" And one of them struck the servant of the high priest and cut off his right ear. But Jesus said, "No more of this!" And he touched his ear and healed him."*

> *Luke 22:47-51*

So in this situation the disciples did ask the Lord what they should do about a pressing matter, but they did not wait for his response. This is why we should be willing to wait on the Lord before we do anything rashly or out of Spirit. Any faithful servant of the Lord who carries a word, or oracle in their heart from God will have patience and peace about it, before they speak. They will not be moved to quick or hasty choices, but wait on the Flow of Life Water to begin.

In conclusion for this chapter: If Jesus is not the root of your entire life and ministry the only tree that will grow in your garden is the Tree of Knowledge of Good and Evil, and you will be content by only knowing information. That being said if you or anyone else partakes of that fruit you will surely die, or someone may in the process. However if Jesus is the root of all that you do, the garden of your heart will spring forth the tree of life and your fruit will be good for all to eat.

Then the angel showed me the river of the water of life, bright as crystal, flowing from the throne of God and of the Lamb through the middle of the street of the city; also, on either side of the river, the tree of life with its twelve kinds of fruit, yielding its fruit each month. The leaves of the tree were for the healing of the nations.

Revelation 22:1-2

This is what our ministry as prophets must look like and genuinely be. The leaves of the tree were for the healing of the nations, not the destruction. We know that Jesus is the True Vine and we must be linked into his Life Flow. If we are not connected to the Ministry of Jesus, we will produce the fruit of another tree, which brings knowledge and death. To which vine is your life connected?

The Holy Spirit is moving all of us
back from Knowledge to Life!
Are you willing to go with him there?
If so, this is where your anointed ministry will produce Life!

CHAPTER EIGHTEEN

Where Is Your Treasure?

When the Holy Spirit moves us from Knowledge to Life, we end up seeing the "Treasure" that is the source of Life. In your ministry, knowing where your treasure is, defines all that you do or say. In this chapter I would like to raise a powerful question, "Where is Your Treasure?" When you bring light to this area in your life, it will clearly show you the inspiration of your entire prophetic ministry. People speak about their treasures, and for us walking prophetically, our Treasure must be clearly understood. So, "Where is your Treasure?", and then the next logical question arrives, "What is your Treasure?" To answer these questions, let's first define the word treasure.

Treasure: (From Webster's Old Edition) "Wealth accumulated; particularly, a stock or store of money in reserve. A great quantity of anything collected for future use. Something very much valued. Great abundance."

God emphatically treasures us "His Creation", and he jealously longs for our fellowship. From the very beginning in the Garden of Eden, God loved walking and talking with his creation, "Mankind". Because God is good, and never changes, he never loses his heart for his special treasure. We are his special treasure! We, on the other hand, are easily swayed by the things of the earth, and our hearts over time begin to treasure things other than God himself. When this happens God moves in zealousness, and righteousness to reclaim his lost treasure back to his heart again. The first story shows God's heart towards us, and reveals his attitude when we treasure something other than him. This story begins in the book of Ezekiel, where the "Prophet Man", became the message of God's heart.

Then this message came to me from the Lord: "Son of Man, with one blow I will take away your dearest treasure. Yet you must not show any sorrow at her death. Do not weep; let there be no tears. Groan silently, but let there be no wailing at her grave. Do not uncover your head, or take off your sandals. Do not perform the usual rituals or mourning, or accept food brought to you by consoling friends." So I proclaimed this to the people the next morning, and in the evening my wife died. The next morning I did everything I had been told to do.

Then the people asked, "What does all this mean? What are you trying to tell us?" So I said to them, "A message came to me from the Lord, and I was told to give this message to the people of Israel. This is what the sovereign Lord says: I will defile my temple, the source of your security and pride, the place your heart delights in. Your sons and daughters whom you left behind in Judea will be slaughtered by the sword. Then you will do as Ezekiel has done. You will not mourn in public or console yourselves by eating the food brought by friends. Your heads will remain covered, and your sandals will not be taken off. You will not mourn or weep, but you will waste away because of your sins. You will mourn privately for all the evil you have done. Ezekiel is an example for you; you will do just as he has done. And when that time comes, you will know that I am the sovereign Lord." Then the Lord said to me, "Son of man, on the day I take away their stronghold-their joy, and glory, their hearts desire, their dearest treasure- I will also take away their sons and daughters. And on that day a survivor from Jerusalem will come to you in Babylon, and tell you what has happened. And when he arrives, your voice will suddenly return, so you can talk to him, and you will be a symbol for these people. Then they will know that I am the Lord.

Ezekiel 24:15-27 (NLT)

The glory of the people of Israel at this time was their temple. This had become their greatest boast, and greatest desired treasure. God used Ezekiel and took away his special treasure (his wife), as an example to demonstrate where our First Treasure should belong. We should not assume by this text that Ezekiel had misguided love for his wife, and it may be wrong to do so. But we can say that he was used as an example to the children of Israel, that they had misguided placement of their special treasure. God was not happy by a people who turned away from him, to their own hand made glories. This temple, it's glory, worship, pomp and circumstance had rapidly become an idol, and a treasure other than God himself. When a treasure is anything other than our Creator God Almighty, it is a misplaced treasure. For the next example let's look at a parable that Jesus spoke in the book of Luke.

And he told them a parable, saying, "The land of a rich man produced plentifully, and he thought to himself, 'What shall I do, for I have nowhere to store my crops?' And he said, 'I will do this: I will tear down my barns and build larger ones, and there I will store all my grain and my goods. And I will say to my soul, "Soul, you have ample goods laid up for many years; relax, eat, drink, be merry."

But God said to him, 'Fool! This night your soul is required of you, and the things you have prepared, whose will they be?' So is the one who lays up treasure for himself and is not rich toward God.

Luke 12:16-21

The answer to this above parable is simply defined by the following scripture found in Ecclesiastes. The answer is, everything treasured other than God is vanity.

I made great works. I built houses and planted vineyards for myself. I made myself gardens and parks, and planted in them all kinds of fruit trees. I made myself pools from which to water the forest of growing trees. I bought male and female slaves, and had slaves who were born in my house. I had also great possessions of herds and flocks, more than any who had been before me in Jerusalem. I also gathered for myself silver and gold and the treasure of kings and provinces. I got singers, both men and women, and many concubines, the delight of the sons of man. So I became great and surpassed all who were before me in Jerusalem. Also my wisdom remained with me. And whatever my eyes desired I did not keep from them. I kept my heart from no pleasure, for my heart found pleasure in all my toil, and this was my reward for all my toil. Then I considered all that my hands had done and the toil I had expended in doing it, and behold, all was vanity and a striving after wind, and there was nothing to be gained under the sun.

Ecclesiastes 2:4-11

The problem is most people live, function, and interact with the world differently than how God intends for us to do. If you are an American, you will often hold tightly to the dream of happiness that is so vainly portrayed to everyone. If you are materialistic, you will be focused on every new movie, gadget, or worldly goods to better your "living" on earth. Many Christians have horribly left the narrow path for a broader more complacent path of selfish indulgence and desire. The Bible here again clearly illustrates this type of thinking to us in the following verses.

> *...from men by your hand, O LORD, from men of the world whose portion is in this life. You fill their womb with treasure; they are satisfied with children, and they leave their abundance to their infants...*

> *Psalms 17:14*

> *Come now, you rich, weep and howl for the miseries that are coming upon you. Your riches have rotted and your garments are moth-eaten. Your gold and silver have corroded, and their corrosion will be evidence against you and will eat your flesh like fire. You have laid up treasure in the last days. Behold, the wages of the laborers who mowed your fields, which you kept back by fraud, are crying out against you, and the cries of the harvesters have reached the ears of the Lord of hosts. You have lived on the earth in luxury and in self-indulgence. You have fattened your hearts in a day of slaughter.*

> *James 5:1-5*

To clarify what is being explained in this chapter, we need to see that it is about the heart, not about how much money/wealth you have. All of these scriptural applications are based on heart matters, and this is my focus. For the scripture clearly says:

> *Do not lay up for yourselves treasures on earth, where moth and rust destroy and where thieves break in and steal, but lay up for yourselves treasures in heaven, where neither moth nor rust destroys and where thieves do not break in and steal. For where your treasure is, there your heart will be also.*

> *Matthew 6:19-21*

That being said...

For the Gentiles seek after all these things, and your heavenly Father knows that you need them all. But seek first the kingdom of God and his righteousness, and all these things will be added to you.

Matthew 6:32-33

If you hold your treasure with God's perspective, it is placed in God's hands. If you are building your storehouse here on the earth, your life and words will start to reflect a treasure that will perish this side of eternity. Many people pursue earthly treasures that amount to nothing at the end of their life. They build worthless empires to only leave them desolate when they die. Anything, that becomes a treasure to you other than God himself, is of no eternal value. This is what some of our modern "False Treasures" look like in our society today. People treasure many of the following: Talent, music, clothing, relationships, worldly possessions, words, speakers, sermons, preachers, and numerous other carnal expressions of nothingness.

Many who call themselves Christians know more about the ways of the world, than they do about the ways of God. These so called "Christians" have placed priority on natural man made things, or man used things. The Bible says that we should have "No other gods before Him !" (Exodus 20:3). Yet, how many times do these things come before God in priority? You all know what I am saying, because we all have seen this happen. People exclaim over the praise and worship music on many Sundays, about how good it was, instead of exclaiming the "ONE" we are worshiping. While some may exclaim on how good a particular preacher spoke using eloquent words, instead of lifting high the Word of God. There are yet others who glorify human talent more than the one who gave it to them. When the individual becomes more visible than God, this is a human based treasure. It is all about perspective, if your treasure is in heaven, you will reflect the message of heaven in what you do and how you speak. If your treasure is based on earth, your entire life will represent that perishing, worthless message.

Many people will scoff at this deep word, and suggest that, it is far too radical, or "overly spiritual". Yet the reality is, if Paul, Peter, or Jesus himself walked through our churches, people would be laying flat on the ground because of the convicting word they would share about the current state of Christendom. Again, people's minds have become "Scarred and Numb" to the real depth of the Word of God. To walk correctly with your treasure in Heaven, you must know more about who your treasure actually is! To do that, we once again need to look at the definition of the word Treasure, and this time look at its Greek Origin as well.

Treasure: (From Webster's Old Edition) "Wealth accumulated; particularly, a stock or store of money in reserve. A great quantity of any thing collected for future use. Something very much valued. Great abundance."

Treasure–From the Greek word... "thesauros, pronounced (Thay saw ros)"

Treasure–(From Thayer's)... "the place in which good and precious things are collected and laid up, a casket, coffer, or other receptacle, in which valuables are kept, a treasury, storehouse, repository, magazine, the things laid up in a treasury, collected treasures."

When you look at this background of the word treasure you see very clearly that this is where we get our English word Thesaurus from. This puts a mighty understanding before our eyes to discover. Jesus is The Word of God, Jesus is also our treasure, therefore it can be said that, Jesus is the first Thesaurus! We look at a Thesaurus to get definitions and terminology correct for studying. Therefore when you start to realize the value in this term, you see Jesus so much deeper than before.

The inspired Word of God, is life's only True Thesaurus for anything, and Jesus himself is that Treasure Chest of life for us to dig into. But many do not believe this.

In a society that holds the value of their "words" on a pedestal, we forget that ONLY the word of God is of any real value. His words are the only words that can produce life, heal the wounded, restore the broken, and redeem the lost. Don't waste your time building up your vocabulary for the sake of eloquence and intelligence, rather store up in your hearts God's word and value it above all things. In doing so you will have a treasure worth dying for. Even Paul said the following:

> *For Christ did not send me to baptize but to preach the gospel, and not with words of eloquent wisdom, lest the cross of Christ be emptied of its power.*
>
> *1 Corinthians 1:17*

We have built massive libraries of books, full of content, and worldly wisdom. Yet, not one of these can bring life, or transfer your soul to heaven after it dies, unless we are speaking about the Bible, the Word of God. We fill our brains with the wisdom of the world, and cherish it far above any "simple" thoughts. Yet, the Bible remains steadfast with its simple and true message. While many of the useless books may be a treasure to most people, it's not the real treasure. The Word of God will not perish, every other treasure will perish. That's why we must store up our treasures in the imperishableness of God's word. It is the only word that never fails. Those who treasure Jesus, our thesaurus of God, find a great safety for dwelling. However, most of humanity including many "professing Christians" are doing everything they can to rip off the protective clothes of the Word of God, for a so called "freedom from Legalism". Yet few on the other hand find great safety dwelling IN, and loving every "Jot" and "Tittle" the word of God has to offer them. The word of God is the safest place to make your home. Venture out into the humanistic world some, and soon you will forget how to return home again.

If you are working on a research paper and need a definition for something you will look into a Thesaurus for the correct answer. Yet in life many who are in a difficult situation never stop for one moment to look into our "Holy Thesaurus" which contains every answer to all of our problems. Every answer, every suggestion, and all understanding comes from the Word of God. It is our greatest treasure, and yet many neglect this

"Awesome Treasure", for things of the earth.

If you don't have your treasure in Jesus, you will be swayed by the things of the world. The devil wants you to love and cherish anything but Jesus.

The Bible inspired by Jesus himself through the Holy Spirit, is our greatest treasure, and it has a lot to tell us regarding this treasure we have. Let's take a look now at several verses from scripture that remind us of our "Safe Haven" in the Word of God!

> *The LORD is exalted, for he dwells on high; he will fill Zion with justice and righteousness, and he will be the stability of your times, abundance of salvation, wisdom, and knowledge; the fear of the LORD is Zion's treasure.*
>
> *Isaiah 33:5-6*

> *The good person out of his good treasure brings forth good, and the evil person out of his evil treasure brings forth evil.*
>
> *Matthew 12:35*

> *The young man said to him, "All these I have kept. What do I still lack?" Jesus said to him, "If you would be perfect, go, sell what you possess and give to the poor, and you will have treasure in heaven; and come, follow me." When the young man heard this he went away sorrowful, for he had great possessions.*
>
> *Matthew 19:20-22*

> *By faith Moses, when he was grown up, refused to be called the son of Pharaoh's daughter, choosing rather to be mistreated with the people of God than to enjoy the fleeting pleasures of sin. He considered the reproach of Christ greater wealth than the treasures of Egypt, for he was looking to the reward.*

Hebrews 11:24-26

The good person out of the good treasure of his heart produces good, and the evil person out of his evil treasure produces evil, for out of the abundance of the heart his mouth speaks. "Why do you call me 'Lord, Lord,' and not do what I tell you?

Everyone who comes to me and hears my words and does them, I will show you what he is like: he is like a man building a house, who dug deep and laid the foundation on the rock. And when a flood arose, the stream broke against that house and could not shake it, because it had been well built. But the one who hears and does not do them is like a man who built a house on the ground without a foundation. When the stream broke against it, immediately it fell, and the ruin of that house was great.

Luke 6:45-49

One of the ways to treasure God more, is to know that he has treasured us first. We love him, because He has first loved us. When we were born again we were given his life, and very words to live by. Jesus has implanted his Spiritual DNA in our lives to produce life for others. The Word says:

For God, who said, "Let light shine out of darkness," has shone in our hearts to give the light of the knowledge of the glory of God in the face of Jesus Christ. But we have this treasure in jars of clay, to show that the surpassing power belongs to God and not to us."

2 Corinthians 4:6-7

Therefore put away all filthiness and rampant wickedness and receive with meekness the implanted word, which is able to save your souls.

James 1:21

What an awesome privilege it is to be trusted with such a valuable treasure, in such weak vessels! Glory to God, and Hallelujah, that he delights to pour into us a new DNA of His Glory. When you live on this planet you will see only two types of DNA, one is the Spiritual DNA of Jesus Christ, and the other is the DNA of the World. If the treasure of God is implanted in you, you will be bearing the fruit of his Kingdom. If you contain the treasure of the world, your fruit will be blemished, perishable, and without eternal value. This is why God wants us to give him our full hearts to put his full treasure in. If we try to hold onto the things of this world we will not leave room for the treasure of God to dwell in us. You can't put two types of treasure in this storage unit of our body. It's one or the other, there is not room for both. Yet many people try to live storing treasure from both.

Those who have the Spiritual DNA of Jesus are the same who also store up their eternal treasures in heaven. This treasure consists of: Mercy, Salvation, Love, redemption, hope of glory, and all that is in Jesus. These are the ones who have absolutely nothing on this earth. They have given up all for the sake of Christ and picked up their cross to follow him. Those who have the worlds DNA, have stored up their treasure on earth. These treasures will all perish in the end of time. These things that they put their trust in have no eternal significance, yet in heaven wrath still remains for them, because they have not fully trusted in Jesus. These are those who rejected Jesus and sent him away on his cross. They chose the comfort of this world for a season, and rejected the one who could give them comfort for all of eternity.

We are called to shine the light of truth on people's "so called"Treasures, to show them the insignificance of what they value, in comparison to who Jesus is. The hope in doing so is that they will cast away all that is worthless in repentance, and believe on the one who is the "True Treasure of Heaven". Your ministry as a prophet is a ministry of redemption and life, filled with the truth of who God is. If you partake of the treasures on this side of eternity your words and speech will reflect an inadequate ministry. However, leaving a life of comfort, for a hard road of trials is never an easy task, but we must know where our Real Treasure is, and this is the entire backbone of pure ministry. If you know where your treasure really is, you will not fall prey to: Apathy, complacency, worldliness, indifference, and the cares of this life. These are all dangers, and he who treasures something other than God's word, walks down a clear path of destruction. You must at all costs embrace entirely the treasure God has implanted in you, and carry it looking forward to eternity, where you full treasure remains.

In conclusion let us be exhorted by these following verses to remind us of what happens when we reach eternity.

> *For no one can lay a foundation other than that which is laid, which is Jesus Christ. Now if anyone builds on the foundation with gold, silver, precious stones, wood, hay, straw each one's work will become manifest, for the Day will disclose it, because it will be revealed by fire, and the fire will test what sort of work each one has done. If the work that anyone has built on the foundation survives, he will receive a reward. If anyone's work is burned up, he will suffer loss, though he himself will be saved, but only as through fire. Do you not know that you are God's temple and that God's Spirit dwells in you? If anyone destroys God's temple, God will destroy him. For God's temple is holy, and you are that temple. Let no one deceive himself. If anyone among you thinks that he is wise in this age, let him become a fool that he may become wise. For the wisdom of this world is folly with God. For it is written, "He catches the wise in their craftiness," and again, "The Lord knows the thoughts of the wise, that they are futile.*
>
> *1 Corinthians 3:11-20*

When your treasure is Jesus, "The Word of God", much of your works will not be burned away by the fires of Heaven's Judgment (for Christians). But if you are actively investing in treasures of no eternal value, it will be a sad day for you at this judgment. Many don't think it is possible to live in this world, yet not of it, but Jesus truly gave us his life as an example, along with our great cloud of witnesses that have walked before us. When you walk after God investing fully in Him, your life will reflect the great treasure waiting for you on the other side of eternity.

Finally to close, let us be encouraged by a verse that has been already quoted in this chapter once again. But this time let's look at it from Jesus' perspective. Luke 12:34 says, "For where your treasure is, there will your heart be also." These are the very words of Jesus, and if you see his heart, this will fill you with such a measure of love you can't contain it. We are His treasure, and that means his heart is towards us, and our ministry. How can we waste our time here on the earth, when Jesus is deeply waiting for jars of clay to reveal his glory? Truly those who know their God, and the Treasure in him, will reflect a sold out life for his kingdom! If you do not know this, you will drift easily onto the broad road that so many other "Christians" walk down. Our path is a narrow path, let's join Jesus on it.

> *...and the knowledge of God's mystery, which is Christ, in whom are hidden all the treasures of wisdom and knowledge.*
>
> *Colossians 2:2b-3*

> *Jehovah is exalted, for He dwells on high; He has filled Zion with justice and righteousness. And He will be the security of your times, strength of salvation, wisdom, and knowledge; the fear of Jehovah is His treasure.*
>
> *Isaiah 33:5-6 (LITV)*

> *Is Jesus truly your Treasure, your pearl of great price? If so then your life will clearly reflect it, and there will be no mistake about where your treasure is!*

CHAPTER NINETEEN

Pointing People to Jesus!

It is one thing to know where and who your treasure is; it is another thing to help people arrive at that Treasure. That is why this main final chapter is about helping people to arrive at Jesus. Jesus is the end of all true prophetic ministry! Whether it's in a word you speak, or in a sermon you preach, the outcome of all your prophetic messages should bring people to the feet of Jesus.

> *Then I fell down at his feet to worship him, but he said to me, "You must not do that! I am a fellow servant with you and your brothers who hold to the testimony of Jesus. Worship God." For the testimony of Jesus is the spirit of prophecy.*
>
> *Revelation 19:10*

Do you remember when you first met Jesus in your own life? What was your state of being at that time? Were you like the prodigal son, or were you like the woman caught in adultery? Perhaps you could have been like Nicodemus, or like one of the disciples. You may have been on your sick bed, or sitting under a tree when you found Jesus. Regardless at some point you encountered Jesus for the first time, and it changed everything in your life! This is the foundation for all of your ministry whether it is prophetic or evangelistic. Revealing Jesus to the church and the world is the heart of all that we do in ministry. When you have sat at the feet of Jesus long enough, you will know his character, and know his voice. If you have not arrived at Jesus, your ministry will not reflect the Spirit Life or his heart.

The question must be asked, "What does your purpose in prophetic ministry look like?" Some may think it is the following: Calling down fire from heaven, shutting up the sky so it doesn't rain, pronouncing a curse over sinners, having your picture on large billboards, sounding spiritual with your words of "Knowledge", having amazing dreams, or visions, foretelling the future, rebuking masses of people, or any other numerous things? It doesn't matter the means of your prophetic ministry as much as it matters the Message of your prophetic ministry. Prophetic expressions will vary, and as it has been previously stated prophetic ministry differs now in the New Covenant.. But the Message will always point people to Jesus.

Prophets should point people to: his life, his salvation, his holiness, his love, his redemption, his faithfulness, his character, his promises, his hope and glory, his restoration, simply everything that is the being and character of Prophetic ministry points to Jesus, at ALL TIMES. Yet many in our society have wandered away from the message of Jesus in Prophetic Ministry, and walked in the way of "Self Expression". This type of ministry will always lead people to the minister himself, causing a blockade to Jesus. When God saved you and redeemed you to be a vessel or tool for his purposes, he did not plan on you sharing the glory with him in any way. Though we have light shined on us because of him, Christ shares his glory with no man. Yet many have stepped into the limelight, and partaken in what is not theirs to have.

In the last 100 years, self-expression and humanism rule our society.

People wear name tags of their "Spiritual Gifts" and proclaim "Their Calling" and flaunt their "talents". It is a sad shame when a man or woman gets in the limelight only reserved for Jesus. The Apostolic Gift then precedes their name instead of "follower of Jesus". It becomes, pastor so and so, prophet so and so, Evangelist so and so, and yet so many years ago they simply had the title of Christian. We need to once again return to be fellow believers instead of "apostolic" peddlers. Seriously what are we advertising here, ourselves, or Jesus? I am not in any way saying it's wrong to have the apostolic gifts, or ministry of the spirit, but what I am saying is this, "it is wrong if YOU become the focus and not JESUS!" Oh how sad it is to see so many churches today look like this individuality of personality. If we get in the way, then people will not arrive at Jesus. This is one of the greatest problems going on in many of our current churches.

Our society filled with humanism, has helped facilitate this rampant problem. Look at it: we have personal social networks (which I will leave unnamed, but you know to what I refer to here) that are all about "ME"!" What I am wearing, what I am doing, where I am going, what my dog did, what I am thinking, what my cat did, what my son did at baseball, what my wife said, what time I got up, what time I made my bed, my my my my my my my, me me me me ME! In essence we are broadcasting ourselves over the internet every minute of the day. It's all about me! Unfortunately this is extremely visible in our church congregations as well. Self has returned to the great throne of life, and Jesus is put in the co-pilot seat. This lifestyle of self expression, has given our flesh and self nature large reigns. Though this media does have the potential to reach people for God's kingdom work, unfortunately in many cases, it does not.

We as leaders, or followers, must always be aware of how dangerous our flesh nature is. The Spirit fights with our flesh, because our flesh wants to be LORD. If self is on the throne people will see you. If Jesus is on your throne people will see Jesus. But it's hard to deny yourself in a society like this, where self is patronized, and pampered.

This is why the true road of Christianity is often a nameless and faceless one. We should make note of any church or system that feels otherwise.

Beware of churches and denominations who "showcase" or "promenade" their leaders. For this is NOT the true essence and life of Jesus Christ! For Jesus Christ came not to be on display, but to serve. And if a leader is on display, what truly is the message and spirit behind what they say? The only thing we should see on display is the authentic life of Jesus Christ. We should not see a person, a pastor, or a musician. While true it may be, that they take a place of ministry, they are only vessels TO-> the glory of God, and should truly be non-existent to our natural eyes. If we see them with natural affections, then they have gotten in the way of the cross of Jesus. If we allow ourselves to be visible, and on "DISPLAY", then we will have fallen into the same trap as the Devil did in his sin. For he stopped and looked at himself, and thought of his own appearance. The minute we look at ourselves (like the devil did) is the minute we stop reflecting Jesus' glory. We have glory on us, because Jesus shines through us. There is no light whatsoever that originates in our flesh. It all originates from the throne of Jesus Christ. We should never let the praise from man stop upon us.

The goal of any words that a New Covenant prophet speaks should cause the hearers to arrive at Jesus and not himself. Let's take a look at one of the best examples in scripture that reveals this attitude of selfless prophetic ministry. We will look at the life of John the Baptist "The Prophet".

> *And this is the testimony of John, when the Jews sent priests and Levites from Jerusalem to ask him, "Who are you?" He confessed, and did not deny, but confessed, "I am not the Christ." And they asked him, "What then? Are you Elijah?" He said, "I am not." "Are you the Prophet?" And he answered, "No." So they said to him, "Who are you? We need to give an answer to those who sent us. What do you say about yourself?" He said, "I am the voice of one crying out in the wilderness, 'Make straight the way of the Lord,' as the prophet Isaiah said.*

> *(Now they had been sent from the Pharisees.) They asked him, "Then why are you baptizing, if you are neither the Christ,*

nor Elijah, nor the Prophet?" John answered them, "I baptize with water, but among you stands one you do not know, even he who comes after me, the strap of whose sandal I am not worthy to untie." These things took place in Bethany across the Jordan, where John was baptizing. The next day he saw Jesus coming toward him, and said, "Behold, the Lamb of God, who takes away the sin of the world! This is he of whom I said, 'After me comes a man who ranks before me, because he was before me.' I myself did not know him, but for this purpose I came baptizing with water, that he might be revealed to Israel." And John bore witness: "I saw the Spirit descend from heaven like a dove, and it remained on him. I myself did not know him, but he who sent me to baptize with water said to me, 'He on whom you see the Spirit descend and remain, this is he who baptizes with the Holy Spirit.' And I have seen and have borne witness that this is the Son of God." The next day again John was standing with two of his disciples, and he looked at Jesus as he walked by and said, "Behold, the Lamb of God!" The two disciples heard him say this, and they followed Jesus. Jesus turned and saw them following and said to them, "What are you seeking?" And they said to him, "Rabbi" (which means Teacher), "where are you staying?" He said to them, "Come and you will see." So they came and saw where he was staying, and they stayed with him that day, for it was about the tenth hour.

John 1:19-39

Now it is unsure how long Andrew and John (the brother of James) were walking with John the Baptist in his ministry. But if you really look at these verses carefully, you will see what a prophet goes through in ministry. John the Baptist said, "Behold the Lamb". The next verses state, "And they followed Jesus." This is such a beautiful picture of all true prophetic ministry. Hallelujah! Perhaps if I attempt to scratch the bottom and pull a deeper meaning we all could assume John the Baptist might have been saddened by this turn of events where he lost "his" disciples. But I hardly think that this was the case for him. John knew the Lamb of God, and the Power of God, and he was happy, but he was indeed a man, and might have potentially suffered sadness from their leaving. Yet when we see Andrew and John leave to follow Jesus, it is at this moment that we get a glimpse of the pains of the "cross life". If we continue on by looking at some more verses from his life, we can see how his heart felt about the ministry of Jesus.

> John also was baptizing at Aenon near Salim, because water was plentiful there, and people were coming and being baptized (for John had not yet been put in prison). Now a discussion arose between some of John's disciples and a Jew over purification. And they came to John and said to him, "Rabbi, he who was with you across the Jordan, to whom you bore witness—look, he is baptizing, and all are going to him." John answered, "A person cannot receive even one thing unless it is given him from heaven. You yourselves bear me witness, that I said, 'I am not the Christ, but I have been sent before him.' The one who has the bride is the bridegroom. The friend of the bridegroom, who stands and hears him, rejoices greatly at the bridegroom's voice. Therefore this joy of mine is now complete. He must increase, but I must decrease.
>
> *John 3:23-30*

By this time more disciples had come to follow John again in his ministry of baptism and repentance. Yet in these few verses we see the key to his joy, and the goal of all prophetic ministry. It is all found in these above verses. "He must increase, but I must decrease!" We are friends of God, and lovers of Jesus, it is our joy to point people to Jesus. We may have seasons of congregations, or followers, yet the reality is that we must not get in the way of these people coming to Jesus. If the people stop at us, we have failed entirely in our ministry. How desperately horrible our society (including "church society") has become when it comes to attention towards ourselves. People must come to us, and go through us to Jesus. If they stop and wait at our feet, we have missed the standard of Jesus Christ.

People should be able to grow wherever they are, as a result of our true prophetic ministry. If they have to follow us around the nation and world to get milk and meat, we have not ministered the Gospel because the Lord is capable of maturing any believer, anywhere by the Power of the Holy Spirit. Our ministry is not about collecting followers on this side of eternity, it is about ushering people to Jesus. People are going to arrive at Jesus one way or another, and by that I mean either now or in eternity. If they arrive at Jesus now it will be during this season of Mercy. Because Jesus is sitting on the mercy seat currently and he wants all to come to him in salvation. But if we do not do our jobs faithfully as ministers, people may miss the call of Christ, and arrive at Jesus while he is sitting on the Great White Throne of Judgment. This is the clear reality of why prophetic ministry is both a ministry of restoration and redemption. We are to restore things in error in the body, and redeem those who are not in the body.

John the Baptist gives us an amazing testimony of pointing people to Jesus during his ministry of repentance. It brought him joy to usher people on to Jesus away from himself. So too, we should be exceedingly happy when others meet Jesus because of our ministry, and then grow with him from there. Our goal is not to make disciples of ourselves, our goal is to make disciples of Jesus. Beware of any church or para-church ministry that makes disciples of "their system". Our command is to make disciples of Jesus, at ALL TIMES!

Another danger we should avoid stems from people calling attention to your ministry. We should not be on a pedestal, and if we are not careful the focus will easily turn off of Jesus and on to you. God makes a very clear case in point about this in Scripture. Let's look at the mistake of Peter to further see this illustrated.

> *And after six days Jesus took with him Peter and James, and John his brother, and led them up a high mountain by themselves. And he was transfigured before them, and his face shone like the sun, and his clothes became white as light. And*

behold, there appeared to them Moses and Elijah, talking with him. And Peter said to Jesus, "Lord, it is good that we are here. If you wish, I will make three tents here, one for you and one for Moses and one for Elijah." He was still speaking when, behold, a bright cloud overshadowed them, and a voice from the cloud said, "This is my beloved Son, with whom I am well pleased; listen to him." When the disciples heard this, they fell on their faces and were terrified.

Matthew 17:1-6

The mistake of Peter happened when he said, "I will make three tents here..." Yet God quickly and emphatically revealed his heart about Peter's comments. God said from heaven, "This is my beloved Son, with whom I am well pleased, LISTEN TO HIM!" (emphasis mine). The focus wasn't Moses, or Elijah, it was JESUS. There are many different ways to potentially interpret this particular passage, but interpreting it this way does fall in accord with the heart of scripture, because all prophecy and ministry will focus on Jesus ONLY! It's not about the men standing near Jesus, it is about Jesus himself. When we are speaking frequently in ministry, many will have a tendency to bring the attention to "your words" or "your ministry" but you should always bear in the forefront of your mind, that Jesus deserves the outcome of all your hard work as a minister.

In conclusion for this chapter, the truest ministry of any prophetic person will be to draw the hearts of mankind closer to Jesus! We must not be like the Pharisees who paraded and flaunted their status or leadership, desiring to be seen and greeted even in the market places. We must be careful not to make the disciples mistake, when they tried to stop the children from coming to Jesus. Because everyone is welcome to Jesus at all times. Jesus demonstrated that his salvation was reaching to the ends of the earth to all people types, and all types of sinners. Prostitutes, tax collectors, fisherman, Pharisee's, Greeks, Gentiles, Jews, Barbarians, and many common people were all welcome to come to the feet of Jesus, to repent and live.

We must also remember how dangerous and wicked our flesh nature is. Our flesh wants to crawl on top of our throne and rule us and others for its personal gain. Our society feeds this wretched fire of flesh and it will burn out of control if not daily monitored by the Holy Spirit. We are not here to let self reign in control of our lives. While yet we do have creativity, and art, "Our truest art form as Christians is not "Self Expression", it is "Christ Expression". Everything that we do or say must bring people closer to the reality of Jesus Christ. Anything else is a waste of time. Jesus has sent out a call to the world for people to come to him just as they are. Are you helping people get to Jesus, or are you getting in the way?

> *The religious society gets excited when they hear or see talent in someone, but I on the other hand get excited when I hear or see Jesus in someone. Do people see Jesus in your ministry?*

CHAPTER TWENTY

Prologue—Closing Exhortations

Well together we have arrived at the final chapter of my closing thoughts for this book. This final chapter has small individual bullets of information that are in no particular order. But these final sections and thoughts are very important to remember while you proceed towards ministry. I would like to speak as plainly as possible with you talking to you as if you were my own family for these final thoughts. My whole goal is to see the body of Christ functioning correctly, and that includes the arm of prophetic ministry. My hope and prayers are that you thoroughly cling to the Lord Jesus and move by the Spirit for the Redemption and Restoration of the body and humanity in the last days. God has called many of you to walk prophetically and my prayers are that you do it correctly with the mind of the Lord!

The Two Heartbeats: The foundation of your life from day to day depends on which heartbeat you listen to in life. You choose between two heartbeats:. 1. The heartbeat of the Lord. 2. The heartbeat of the devil/

world. The heartbeat of the Lord is a steady, calm, dependable, and totally peaceable heartbeat. His word causes your countenance and life to reflect the confidence of his eternal plans. When you are listening to the Lord's heartbeat in scripture, prayer, and through teachers, you will be able to walk, and live at peace when everything else is falling apart in this world. However if you choose to listen to the heartbeat of the devil/world you will hear a much different sounding heartbeat.

The devil's heartbeat is erratic, inconsistent, and fluctuating. If you spend too much time watching the news, reading the papers, current trends, wars, famines, and rumors of wars, you will take on this heartbeat of trouble and panic. It is very important for your peace to come from the foundational truths of the Bible. I am not saying that watching the news is wrong, but rest assured if you put your ear to that media, and the problems of the earth for a long period of time, your life will reflect uneasiness. People need to hear about the peace of God, and if you have your ear to Jesus's bosom you will reflect that same message of peace. We are living in the last days of the earth, be careful not to get caught up in the rapid declining status of society, governments, countries and earthly disasters. The hope we have is the peace that God has to offer, and we must be able to speak that hope. The peace of the Lord is the salvation call for all mankind to come to Jesus Christ!! Sing the song of peace for others by truly listening to the heartbeat of the Lord.

The Heart of True Prayer: As it has been stated in other chapters, bitterness creeps in so quickly to the life of a prophet by seeing all the problems that are being faced. If bitterness takes a hold in your life, your heart of redeeming prayer may dwindle. One of the clearest signs of a heart of love, is a faithful heart of prayer for these problems that you may see. A heart of prayer is truly a litmus test as to what is going on in your life. People don't often travail in prayer for others because they don't really care for others. If you become bitter, your care and concern for others will fail. If your prayer life is flowing for others, you are loving them more because of the work of Jesus in your own heart. We must be willing to travail in prayers for others, problems, and concerns that are at hand. If you cannot then you must get alone with the Lord and get it fixed, because bitterness will ruin your ministry. Don't be afraid to gently confront a brother or sister about bitterness if you see it. God wants their prayers to travail as well. Even if you become bitter yourself, you are not cut off from God, but he does desire to purge you of bitterness as quickly as possible. David prayed for the salvation and redemption of his enemies, and so we too would do well to see his example before our eyes. If you cannot genuinely pray for someone's freedom or redemption there is a problem in your heart, because God always desires redemption and mercy triumphing over judgment. Keep this litmus test before your heart, and your close companions, and don't let bitterness, un-love, or any non-compassionate prayers flow out from your life. Walking in a heart of True Prayer really reveals that state of your journey with the Lord.

Willing Learners: One of the best suggestions I have for close companions is to find those who are "sold out" for God in all aspects of their life. Don't be exclusive away from others leaving people out of fellowship with you, but protect quality time with you and intimate close companions. These companions are what I am classifying as Willing Learners. This is drawn from the verse in Hebrews that states: ...But exhort one another every day, as long as it is called "today," that none of you may be hardened by the deceitfulness of sin" (Hebrews 3:13).

If you find fellowship with Christians who want to actively pursue the Lord, and be actively exhorted daily, you will be doing well!! This is a blessing from the Lord and is not to be taken lightly. If you want to pursue the Lord with your full heart, don't settle to the standard of others who do not. That also includes some who may be in leadership with this lesser standard. We are called to diligently seek the Lord, and I recommend you find those who desire the same.

If you have the opportunity to dig deeper with these friends then go for it! Having quality friends who are willing learners, will cause you to see the heart of God more. Complacency is one of the biggest dangers to Christianity, and we are called to be active Christians. Even if there are those who do not want to learn daily, or have you speak into their life daily, you may well indeed encourage them to do so, by your example. Willing Learners truly want to hear the heart of God in all matters, and these friends are jewels from Jesus to cherish.

Don't Walk Alone: Continuing from the preceding paragraph, it is vital to walk along side other believers. You are not called to be a lone "wilderness prophet". We are called to walk together with the Body of Christ in prophetic function. Though there may be seasons where you will be trained alone at times (like Moses, Joseph, Paul, etc) God will be in the process of bringing you back to the Body of Christ to function and be joined there. So yes there may be great seasons of dying and death by yourself, but none-the-less you will be brought back to connect with the whole body of Christ Jesus. If you do not join to the body, and function with the body, your life may well dissolve prophetically. This is why the following verse keeps us accountable and grows us in the body. As it says in Proverbs 27:17 "Iron sharpens iron, and one man sharpens another."

I am totally convinced that God by the Holy Spirit could grow anyone alone, if they were by themselves on an island. But the reality is, we are not called to stay on that island, we are called to walk with one another in unity. Because of the animosity towards prophetic ministry, it may cause you to disconnect, and I am encouraging you to do otherwise. You must connect and remain an active part of the Body of Christ. Because of this many of us have seen the benefits of being in intimate fellowship with those of like minds. A person that knows you, even to a very deep spiritual level can speak directly to any dangers creeping into your life. Furthermore conviction can come from those who are close to you and walking in the Lord. These close friends can also bear witness with you for direction in ministry, and this is valuable. Jesus demonstrates this close knit group of intimate fellowship with John, Peter, and James. So to we can walk in this closeness for protection, growth, fellowship, and perseverance. You cannot successfully walk in prophetic ministry in the New Covenant if you isolate yourself and walk alone. Don't walk alone it is a great danger to your ministry!

Don't Be an Angry Prophet: If bitterness is not dealt with in your life, you will become an angry Prophet. Your ministry is about drawing people to the Lord with good Seeds from his word and Law. Our seeds (of the

Word of God) are not ammunition to throw at people hoping they will get saved. Our seeds must be tenderly given so that they will take root in the ground. If people are making an effort to come back to the Lord we must not be throwing seeds at them in the process. Because it is the Loving kindness of the Lord that leads people to repentance. Now if God calls you to preach a fire and brimstone message, then you better do it, but remember redemption and restoration are the forefront of any message like this, not the destruction of man away from God. Once again our seed sowing ministry is not a grenade throwing ministry. As prophetic ministers we are in many ways to be a cup-bearing minister of servant hood. We are giving food and drink to the hungry and thirsty, and we must be able to have a testimony about how that food and drink of the Lord tastes, when we give it. We must know that lovely taste of Jesus, or our words will be shallow and without flavor. Offering food and drink that you haven't truly first tried is a negligent ministry. The heart of it is a ministry of serving people to redemption with the kindness of the Lord, using tender means to get people there. An angry prophet doesn't make a good server in the restaurant of the Lord. However there are some dishes like fire and brimstone messages that burn your mouth when you eat it, but serving this spicy platter in love, will bring redemption. Make no mistake judgment IS coming to the world, therefore your calling as prophetic watchmen is to encourage people to obtain the mercy of the Lord now, before it is too late. Furthermore you must encourage so called Christians to live righteously after the Lord and not to be partakers of worldly nothingness. Doing this without being an angry prophet will bring life. But remember that anger about sin without true love is dangerous in any ministry. Here is a wonderful quote from Henry Blackaby that joins these thoughts.... "It is a travisty to carry a message of love and yet be filled with hatred." Let us not be angry prophets!"

The Narrow Gate of Uncommon Christianity: Lovingly and tenderly I would like to remind you that most of the religious world is walking on the broad path of destruction. We are called to a different path, the narrow path of Jesus which for many is Uncommon Christianity. This path is not a path much traveled and may feel very lonely at times. It's not an easy "escapism" from pain and suffering, it is actually one that will draw to your attention: the face of persecution, the mouth of accusation, and the hand of humiliation. Many will not understand why you walk such a strict path, and will call you narrow minded and hard headed, for your choices and convictions, SO BE IT!

Rocks will be thrown at you from both sides simply, because you have decided to follow Jesus on this Narrow Highway of Holiness. Don't let the rocks stop you. This is a path where grey areas do not exist, because it's a black and white road about righteousness. There will be times that the "winds of this world" will try to sway you off the path, but you must stand firm and look forward to Jesus! Yes, this may be a hard road, but it is also a glorious one! The reward on this side of eternity is to see people embrace the truth, walk this same path, and be transformed into the image of Christ. Though the persecutions may seem to outweigh the reward on this side of eternity, know that your reward in heaven is greater than you can imagine. When you walk on this narrow path, your life's example will glorify God. Finally we cannot be just content with saving people by the masses, we must strive to get them off the broad road of life, even the broad road of religion, and to the narrow path of true Christianity. Christians if indeed they are true followers need to get out of bed with the world and follow Jesus on the narrow path of true Christianity. It is time to walk away from the lawlessness of the world, shed your grave clothes, and carry yourself like a born again believer instead of a person of compromise. If we tenderly take the time to disciple people to be like Jesus, we will have plenty more companions on this narrow path to heaven!

The Final Thought—"The Compliment from Jesus": To close this section, as well as the book, I would like to leave you with this final exhortation. Let's take a look at Matthew 15 to read some verses first.

> *Then Pharisees and scribes came to Jesus from Jerusalem and said, "Why do your disciples break the tradition of the elders? For they do not wash their hands when they eat." He answered them, "And why do you break the commandment of God for the sake of your tradition? For God commanded,*

'Honor your father and your mother,' and, 'Whoever reviles father or mother must surely die.' But you say, 'If anyone tells his father or his mother, "What you would have gained from me is given to God," he need not honor his father.' So for the sake of your tradition you have made void the word of God. You hypocrites! Well did Isaiah prophesy of you, when he said: "'This people honors me with their lips, but their heart is far from me; in vain do they worship me, teaching as doctrines the commandments of men.'"And he called the people to him and said to them, "Hear and understand: it is not what goes into the mouth that defiles a person, but what comes out of the mouth; this defiles a person."

Matthew 15:1-11

Jesus again confronting the arrogant Pharisees brings scripture from the Old Testament to reveal their hearts. This time Jesus uses Isaiah and quotes him as a case against their fake worship and pretense. The key component that is vitally important to bring out in this passage is 4 small words…"Well Did Isaiah Prophesy…" This book can be summed up in these 4 words. The entire goal and hope is that your prophetic ministry will honor the Lord correctly in all that you do or say. All that we do or say for Jesus should bring delight to his heart. We should bring joy to the Holy Spirit by our willingness to speak correctly, in season, and with the right tone. Jesus complimented Isaiah, because he said "WELL DID ISAIAH prophesy!" Knowing that our entire ministry is the testimony of Jesus, my hope and prayer for you is that you do your ministry correctly. Knowing that prophecy starts and ends with Jesus will help you focus your words, prayers, and thoughts correctly. Keeping your tongue guarded and anointed by the Holy Spirit will bring you great victory! Keeping your eyes on Jesus, and seeing the big picture of Salvation will cause your message to reflect the hope God offers to man.

When your journey on this earth is complete, and when you stand before the Lord to have your works judged, it is my hearts desire that you TOO will hear from the Lord, "WELL DID MY SERVANT PROPHESY!"

SCRIPTURE INDEX

CHAPTER 5

John 7:16-17

Isaiah 50:5-6

John 17:1-2

John 5:30

John 14:26

John 15:26

John 16:7-8

John 16:13-15

1 Corinthians 12:27-28

1 Corinthians 14:1-4

1 Corinthians 14:29-32

1 Corinthians 14:37

1 Thessalonians 5:19-21

Matthew 8:5-13

1 Samuel 1:27-28

1 Samuel 2:12 & 17

1 Samuel 2:18-19

1 Samuel 3:1-10

1 Samuel 3:11-18

Romans 13:1-7

Matthew 22:17-21

1 Peter 2:12-17

Matthew 22:36-40

2 Timothy 3:16-17

Matthew 15:1-6

Isaiah 29:13

Colossians 2:6-8

Hebrews 13:17

1 Peter 5:5

John 10:27

CHAPTER 6

1 Corinthians 14:3

2 Timothy 4:1-2

Hebrews 3:13

Ezekiel 13:4-16

Proverbs 27:6

Matthew 7:1-5

Ephesians 5:18-21

1 Corinthians 14:4 & 22

CHAPTER 7

Ephesians 5:1-4

Ephesians 4:29

1 Timothy 6:20-21

James 4:11

Psalms 34:13

1 Peter 3:10-12

Ephesians 5:12

Psalms 4:2

Exodus 5:9

Exodus 20:7

Ephesians 5:4

1 Timothy 1:6-7

Titus 3:9

Matthew 12:36

Ephesians 5:19-20

Colossians 3:16-17

1 Thessalonians 5:11-15

Proverbs 25:11

2 Corinthians 7:1

Matthew 12:34-37

Acts 22:3-9

Philippians 3:4-10

Galatians 1:13-24

John 11:14-27

John 11:24-26

Luke 22:47-51

Revelation 22:1-2

CHAPTER 18

Ezekiel 24:15-27

Luke 12:16-21

Ecclesiastes 2:4-11

Psalms 17:14

James 5:1-5

Matthew 6:19-21

Matthew 6:32-33

Exodus 20:3

1 Corinthians 1:17

Isaiah 33:5-6

Matthew 12:35

Matthew 19:20-22

Hebrews 11:24-26

Luke 6:45-49

2 Corinthians 4:6-7

James 1:21

1 Corinthians 3:11-20

Luke 12:34

Colossians 2:2b-3

Ezekiel 33:5-6

CHAPTER 19

Revelation 19:10

John 1:19-39

John 3:23-30

Matthew 17:1-6

CHAPTER 20

Hebrews 3:13

Proverbs 27:17

Matthew 15:1-11

SOURCE REFERENCES INDEX

Meyers, Rick. E-Sword. Version 10–Rick Meyers, 2013. Free Web Software- All Rights Reserved Worldwide. Web.

King James Concordance Derivitive Work Published in 1769 Public Domain. Web.

Webster's Dictionary of American English Published in 1828 Public Domain. Web.

Thayer's Greek Definitions Published in 1886, & 1889 Public Domain. Web.

Brown Driver Briggs Hebrew Definitions Published in 1906 Public Domain. Web.

Adam Clarke's Commentary On the Bible Published 1810-1826 Public Domain. Web.

Matthew Henry's Commentary on the Whole Bible Published 1708-1714 Public Domain. Web.

Strong, James, and James Strong. The New Strong's Exhaustive Concordance of the Bible: With Main Concordance, Appendix to the Main Concordance.

Key Verse Comparison Chart, Dictionary of the Hebrew Bible, Dictionary of the Greek Testament. Nashville: Thomas Nelson, 1984. Print.

Vines–Expository Dictionary of Old and New Testament Words 1981–Revell Company

United Kingdom by Marshall and Morgan & Scott Publications. Print.

Theological Dictionary of the New Testament (TD) 1985–Eeerdmans

Grand Rapids, Michigan–Reprinted 1997 Author Geoffrey W. Bromiley Edited by Gerhard Kittle, and Gerhard Friedrich. Print.

Websters Dictionary Modern Version–1997–Random House Publishers New York, Toronto. Print.

Schaeffer, Francis A. How Should We Then Live?: The Rise and Decline of Western Thought and Culture. Old Tappan, NJ: F.H. Revell, 1976. Print.

Luther 2003 -Feature Film Video Recording- MGM & Thrivent Financial. DVD.

Amazing Grace 2007 -Feature Film Video Recording- 20th Century Fox & Ingengious. DVD.

Blackaby, Henry & Richard Blackaby–Experiencing God Day By Day. All Rights Reserved. Printed in the United States. Published by Broadman & Holman Publishers, Nashville, Tennessee.

The Call for Character is made available through Watchlight Books, a Division of Watchlight Ministries. For more information about additional books and other media resources you can find Troy Krombholz on the web at WatchlightMinistries.com. You may also contact Troy directly by e-mail at: Troy@watchlightministries.com.

Solo Deo Gloria!

CPSIA information can be obtained at www.ICGtesting.com
Printed in the USA
LVOW10s1439141213

365211LV00003B/5/P